GREAT TRAVELLING DISASTERS

Hugh Vickers and Caroline McCullough

Illustrations by Bernard Cookson

MACMILLAN

First published 1984 by
PAPERMAC
a division of Macmillan Publishers Limited
4 Little Essex Street London WC2R 3LF
and Basingstoke

Associated companies in Auckland, Delhi, Dublin, Gaborone, Hamburg,
Harare, Hong Kong, Johannesburg, Kuala Lumpur, Lagos, Manzini,
Melbourne, Mexico City, Nairobi, New York, Singapore and Tokyo

Printed in Great Britain by
Redwood Burn Limited, Trowbridge, Wiltshire

British Library Cataloguing in Publication Data

Vickers, Hugh
    Great travelling disasters.
    1. Voyages and travels—Anecdotes,
    facetiae, satire, etc.
    I. Title
    910'.207   G163
    ISBN 0–333–37915–2

GREAT TRAVELLING DISASTERS

Also available in Papermac

Great Operatic Disasters
Even Greater Operatic Disasters
Great Country House Disasters

In memory of Caroline McCullough,
my co-author, who died before
we could finish this book
together.

Ch'io mi scordi di te   (Mozart, K. 551)

Acknowledgements

My deepest thanks are due to the following indefatigable travellers: James Reeve, Anthony Short and Rachel Pakenham.

My deepest gratitude also to Jean Watson and James Comerford, and to my dear friend Sophie von Nagel.

My grateful thanks also to Jacqui Craze of Hay-on-Wye for all her help.

Contents

Introduction

This small volume is but a preliminary study of a mighty theme. I hope, in some ten years' time and with the aid of a vast team of research assistants, to produce the definitive account. My format, I must confess, is neither historical nor particularly schematic – travel disasters are a subject not for classification but rather for awestruck meditation.

The immense subject takes us back through the mists of time to the very origins of mankind. Say we accept von Däneken's thesis, whereby we are the descendants of a race of gods from outer space. Well, judging from the various craters and holes he illustrates, we can only assume for starters that a good proportion of the spaceships crashed. Anyway, if the present condition of humanity is anything to go by, an extraterrestrial expedition with earth as its objective must surely be seen as a truly cosmic travel disaster. I have always felt that if, indeed, the gods deliberately selected the earth as a target it must have been as a penal colony, a sort of Botany Bay where only the lowest members of the stellar hierarchy were sent.

Given this heritage, it is no wonder that man has been travelling disastrously ever since. Either, like Moses, he never even makes his promised land or if, like Columbus, he does, it results in Al Capone, Coca Cola, Richard Nixon, the Klu Klux Klan and deep-frozen cherry pie. True, our earliest great travelling hero, Odysseus, left no such fearful legacy but equally absurdly he extricated himself from the most frightful travel disasters, only to return to his own wife, Penelope, whom he found, needless to say, in deadly danger

1

as a result of his wholly unjustified absence. For was his journey, as we used to say in the war, really necessary? No, its atrocious motive was to take part in the brutal sack of one of the greatest cities and civilizations of the ancient world.

Odysseus, however, does introduce us to the modern concept of travel as an individual, as opposed to collective, act of insanity in which the traveller voluntarily gives up the home and family he loves for a tortured, peripatetic existence in which he is sure to lose at least his luggage, quite likely his life, probably his job, certainly his dignity. Even Goethe's little trip to Italy cost him his ministry in Weimar.

As for dignity, consider the recent June 1984 experience of the travel writer, Dervla Murphy. This intrepid lady has survived travelling all over the Himalayas on a bicycle and the Andes on a donkey without a single disaster. But the god of travel had arranged condign punishment for her on her return. The very first day, whilst taking a dip in the naturally ice-cold Blackwater river near her Irish home, she was butted in the back by an infuriated bullock and broke her spine. In fact the poor lady is at present encased in plaster from the waist upwards. But what is interesting, beyond the irony of this accident, is the quality of her reply when asked whether it was not the redness of her naked form which caused the bullock to charge. To this she gave an answer which at once betrayed the true traveller, 'Oh no, he was attracted by the movement of my hands.' You see, like Odysseus, like all great travellers, she cannot accept that an act that others would regard as foolhardy has brought a straightforwardly disastrous consequence.

The traveller doesn't like the laws of cause and effect by which the stay-at-home guide their lives, and always refers to disaster in a light, disparaging way. Here, for instance, speaks another very different traveller. It is 1912, we are in a sumptuous London drawing room, that of one of the Lascelles sisters. Breakfast time. In she floats, copy of *The Times* in hand, and gives it to her husband with the words, 'My dear, there seems to have been a really rather ghastly boating accident.' It took him a minute or two to work out that what she was referring to was, in fact, the sinking of the Titanic.

Again, I asked a traveller friend of mine what it was like being caught in Addis Ababa in the middle of the 1965 revolution. 'Well,' she said, 'there was this one moment when one felt a trifle out of place.' In fact what happened was this. During bumpy camel rides in the interior of the country she had developed a boil on her bottom, the sort of embarrassing affliction made worse by the fact that you can't see it. On checking into that miserable hotel, the Only Available in Addis Ababa, she made straight for the bathroom only to find that the sole mirror was a shaving mirror, placed at a height suitable for the tallest of tall Ethiops. How to reach it? Only one way. Taking off all her clothes, she clambered on to the lavatory seat while turning her posterior towards the mirror, craning her neck to see, like a ballet dancer doing an arabesque. There was a sudden rattle of gunfire outside. She was startled, slipped and fell against the wall, except that it turned out not to be a wall but a blacked-out window. She crashed through and landed stark naked in the war-torn mainstreet of the Ethiopian capital in the middle of the revolution. A trifle out of place? Quite.

But then the real traveller loves being out of place, and the addition of elements of war, revolution or physical violence only enhances his delight. My own half-brother, the late D B H Vickers, was fortunate indeed among the fraternity of real travellers. For twenty years he was actually *paid* as a senior UN official to reel from one travel disaster to another, usually under heavy fire. In Beirut his flat was seized by rebels who opened fire on government forces below. They left, and two minutes later government troops rushed in, ejected my brother and his family and, on the grounds that he had permitted his apartment to be used as a rebel strongpoint, blew the whole place up, complete with all his possessions.

During the Congo crisis in 1964 he helicoptered 700 miles to a jungle clearing to meet a chief whom the offer of guns and

3

'She crashed through and landed stark naked in the war-torn main street of the Ethiopian capital . . .'

gold had converted to an albeit dimly understood form of Marxism. But their discussions were cut short by an angry roar. Ten feet behind them stood an enormous and very hungry-looking lion. But for the promptitude of the helicopter pilot in getting the rotas moving, my brother's peacekeeping effort in Africa might have consumed him – in the most literal sense.

Most disastrous of all his adventures for him, however, was his participation in the United Nations commissions which briefly supervised the affairs of Papua New Guinea between the time the Dutch left and the Australian government was able to assume control. He found himself interestingly doubling up as Foreign Minister, Minister for Culture and Lord Chief Justice. It wasn't long before he was put to the test. A traditional feud erupted between two tribes who lived on each side of an amazingly obscure and unexplored river. My brother, acting in this case as Minister of Defence, sent a small peacekeeping force to separate the combatants, who were busily shooting at each other with poisoned blowpipes. They were herded into large stockades and invited to cool off, which they managed to do in a couple of days. The elaborate peacemaking process began. However, not before a furious formal note arrived from Canberra in which the Australian government asserted that it noted with outrage and horror the latest high-handed act by the UN High Commission with its scandalous violation of the rights of Australian citizens, who had been forcibly prevented from enjoying their traditional tribal pastimes and imprisoned without charge or trial . . . .

Diplomatic Manoeuvres

The last incident brings us to a major theme – diplomacy. Diplomacy is, of course, nothing more than glorified, institutionalized travelling, the disastrous consequences of which can be guaranteed from the start. Those trained in the Foreign Office to speak Spanish are sent to China; the Chinese specialist will find himself in Ecuador. Even in the thirties when Neville Chamberlain kept returning in triumph from those ill-fated journeys to Munich, we sent a Scandinavian specialist to Buenos Aires in order to free Sir Neville Henderson for Berlin (just in time not to prevent World War II).

But diplomacy has always been like that. Let's look back at the past again. Chaucer was a diplomat – he knew what travelling was really like, which is why *The Canterbury Tales* is so delightful: a work of complete fiction, as remote from the miseries of an actual medieval pilgrimage as it is doubtless possible to get. But Boccaccio is more realistic. Let me give you in brief form, therefore, one of his stories, to my mind the quintessence of diplomatic travel, disasters and all.

One day, the Bishop of Arezzo decided to send an important message to the Archbishop of Siena. It would have been of a political nature – the possibility of an invasion by Papal troops perhaps. He asked his entourage to find the necessary messengers but to his great alarm they were all out in the field, *en route* to Venice, Bologna, Naples . . . . 'Well, Siena's not far. At least find a couple of men who can ride a horse.' This they did; two astonished peasants, in town to sell their produce, soon found themselves in the episcopal presence. Their instructions were clear – they were to learn the message by heart because it was too secret to commit to paper (it was also in Latin so they couldn't understand it) and they would then be given a substantial sum in gold, with twice as much waiting on their return.

Since this was considerably more money than they had ever seen in their lives, they buckled down with a will to the task of learning the message. In a couple of hours they had mastered it to the bishop's satisfaction, collected the gold and, mounted on a couple of splendid horses, set off with a flourish on the dusty road to Siena. Five miles later they started feeling thirsty and decided to pay a visit to one of the many old inns which line that exquisite route even today. One thing leads to another – their journey soon takes on the nature of a glorified pub crawl, a hymn to Orvieto, Montepulciano and that most splendid of local wines, Est Est Est. It is only at about their fifth stop that one turns to the other and says, 'Giuseppe, you know the strangest thing? I've completely forgotten that message we're supposed to deliver.' 'How odd, I can't remember it either.' 'But you must – you are the real messenger. I was merely sent to ride along with you.' 'No, you . . .,' 'No, you . . .,' and so on. But this typically Tuscan argument fizzles out after a very short time. They have to face up to the fact that both have forgotten the message. What to do?

An old Tuscan adage advises one to consider any decision first drunk then sober. True to this they make for the next *osteria* and order a tremendous meal. Surely they must remember the message either in their cups or alternatively in the cruel sobriety of dawn. Yet a few more litres of Orvieto bring no more inspiration – they stagger to bed drunk but slightly fearful.

The next morning brings one of the worst hangovers in human history – but still no message. As they continue their progress from inn to inn, time, as so often happens in travel, seems at first to slow down and then suddenly, as Siena approaches, to speed up alarmingly. Again, as with all travel, the main sense of responsibility, in this case the message, simply ceases to be important. Even had the message possessed any objective meaning, however vital – for instance in modern terms something which might have prevented nuclear war – it would by this time have become wholly irrelevant.

By the time Siena looms up in the distance they are men quite transformed. Of course they don't know what to do but it doesn't seem to matter that much. After every travelling disaster one always starts analysing but this is invariably quite ineffective. Here they think: we can't go back, we can't go on and we can't go anywhere else because if we do they will hunt us down and hang us in the public square. While none of these alternatives seem to have much significance, the best is obviously to go on.

They have a new courage. Travel can imbue you with passionate courage. They ride down the hill and dismount, walk into the Guidoriccio room and fall on their knees in front of the archbishop, who is enthroned in state. 'My lord,' they say, 'we are men from Arezzo.' 'What, from Arezzo? But your arrival is providential. It so happens that I have the most urgent message to send to the Bishop of Arezzo.' 'But, my lord, we had an important message from the Bishop of Arezzo to you.' 'Pah, nothing at all. I'm not interested in his message, some trivial matter of church administration no doubt. No, what counts is my message. Look here,' he says to his servants, 'these men have come all the way from Arezzo. They are tired, hungry, desperately thirsty, utterly exhausted. Give them the best room in the palace.'

The next morning they set off. They have the new message and lots more gold. But it only takes the first stop in the first village for them to have to admit that they have already forgotten it. This time it matters even less. At every inn they reach they are now seen as important messengers, returning from a vital mission. By the time they reach Arezzo they are feeling the sort of level of highness you get, for example, from drinking whisky on an international jet flight. 'What shall we do? Say that we have forgotten both messages? I'm afraid we've had it, but it's been fun anyway.' You know *that* feeling.

Again they go into the bishop's palace, again they fall on their knees, but the bishop rises to his feet and says, 'Oh my God, it's not you two again! ' 'Yes, my lord bishop, we have come back from Siena.' 'Did you deliver the message?' 'No, my lord, we did not.' 'Thank goodness for that,' cries the bishop. 'The entire political situation has changed. Your delivery of the message would have been fatal! In fact, in view of your masterly handling of the situation, I have decided to appoint you both as permanent ambassadors.'

This, of course, is not really a travelling disaster but rather one of the very rare travelling successes. It certainly reveals a great deal about the nature of diplomacy, so often dependent on inadequate messengers. Take, for instance, Sir George Buchanan's telegram to the Foreign Office at the beginning of World War I. In the twenty-four hours which preceded the war the British cabinet was waiting with bated breath for a comment from their ambassador in St Petersburg. Unfortunately, he had recently done a lot of travelling and was even more out of touch with reality than usual. He had quite forgotten that a comment from him might be crucial to the cabinet in their war/peace deliberations. However, at the last moment, he did manage to make a despatch. Decoded in the Foreign Office, it was rushed to Downing Street, where the cabinet was in emergency session under Mr Asquith. It turned out to be a request for a box of chocolates to be sent to his wife . . . .

To take a modern example of disastrous diplomatic travelling, we might mention a recent foreign minister. In an important initiative, he visited both Egypt and Israel in the same trip with a stop at Cyprus in between. The only problem was that he underestimated the tiring nature of this tremendous schedule. By the time he arrived in Cairo he had somehow got his two main cities mixed up. Addressing a very important collection of Arab dignitaries, he began, 'As I stand here in this sacred shrine of the Jewish faith . . . . ' But at least he realized his error and managed to slam into his other speech before his astonished hosts were able to protest.

It is usually American diplomatic representatives whom travelling really gets to. In fact, American travellers as a whole are rather odd. Maybe being American they feel that their forebears have travelled quite enough already anyway. But I don't think that a diplomat of any other nation could have behaved exactly like Mrs Clare Booth Luce on her appointment to the Rome Embassy and the Vatican. She arrived in Rome after a particularly tiring flight and immediately went for her first audience with the Pope, then Pius XII. For some three hours she delivered to him the speech she had carefully prepared on the plane. It was along these lines: 'Momentous historic occasion . . . . the first American woman ambassador . . . . the first US representative to the Vatican of any kind. I mean, your Holiness, I represent in part the aspirations of fifty million Catholics in America . . . . I mean, Catholicism is so important in the world today . . . . Catholicism perhaps might be the only possible bastion against that terrible, evil, awful thing, Communism . . . . ' At this point, Pius XII, unable to stand any more of this tautological clap-trap, simply said, 'Madam, I fully agree with all you say but I think I should remind you that, as a matter of fact, I am a Catholic too.'

At least, however, Mrs Luce's mission was successful, indeed memorable. Let us contrast it with another United States diplomatic mission, a travelling disaster almost unique in its horror, widely known at the time as the 'Gigolo incident'. This practically ruptured relations between the United States and Iran, at one of the most delicate moments of the Shah's reign.

What happened was this. A team of high-powered American politicians and economists, led by Senator Javits, flew out to Teheran via Paris and Baghdad for extremely important bilateral economic talks. Included among their number was my informant, the charming Mrs Albert Brockman of

Long Island, who was brought along as 'a cultural ornament', as she put it. Mrs Brockman is inseparable from her little black poodle, Gigolo; you cannot have one without the other. The flight was, of course, fraught with every kind of disaster and delay. They finally left Baghdad eleven hours late to find, however, that Iranian hospitality had not let them down. The immaculate guard of honour had been reassembled and was at attention on the tarmac behind the resplendent figure of His Imperial Majesty the Shah. The aircraft doors opened and the stairs and red carpet rushed into place. But, alas, just as Senator Javits prepared to lead his delegation out, the unforeseen occurred. Gigolo, who hadn't had a pee since Baghdad, charged out of the plane, down the steps and on to Persian soil where he immediately sought the nearest tree. Unfortunately, the splendidly erect figure of the Shah fitted this bill to perfection and the King of Kings found himself standing rigidly to attention while Gigolo's ample effluent filled his shoes.

(I fear it probably gave His Majesty little comfort to reflect that he was the victim of the worst American diplomatic *commencement de mission* since a United States ambassador to Madrid in the twenties sent one of the hot water bottles he manufactured to the Queen of Spain with a note reading: 'Hope this will keep you warm, honey, when Alfie's away'.)

But this was only the beginning of the Gigolo incident. Next day came the formal reception and banquet, attended by the entire court, cabinet, *corps diplomatique* and anyone else who could bribe their way in. Mrs Brockman was late as usual. (She is always late.) She charged up the palace stairs, clutching Gigolo in her arms. But this was the wrong staircase. At the top, immense double doors loomed. She flung them open, and some five hundred people, all keyed up for the Shah, bowed, curtseyed, in some cases even flung themselves on their knees. Seconds later, the double doors at the other end of the room opened as His Imperial Majesty, the King of Kings, found his entire court and guests with their backs to him, bowing and scraping to an elegant New

'. . . while Gigolo's ample effluent filled his shoes . . .'

York Jewess who, incredibly, was clutching in her arms the hated, loathsome Gigolo. The student of contemporary history will do well to ponder this incident in the context of the deterioration of United States/Iran relations.

Of course, to see diplomatic absurdity elevated to the ultimate level, one must go to Geneva, a city best described as a collective travelling disaster. Geneva's heart lies in the great Palais des Nations, the central chamber of the old League of Nations. On its soaring concrete façade, typical of the early thirties, is incised in giant letters the legend: 'The Nations must disarm or perish' (how typical that so far they have done neither).

The whole scene – the blue lake, the triumphant marble pillars, the strutting peacocks on the lawn – transport one back to the world of those desperately idealistic disarmament conferences held in the twenties: Locarno 1928, for instance. Yet even that was a scene of one of the most glorious travel disasters of all time. You see, there wasn't room in Locarno for the innumerable delegates, teams of experts, special sub-committees and all the residual para-phernalia that attends a major conference. There was, however, extensive accommodation at Stresa, a little way down the shore of Lake Maggiore. The only minor detail which Geneva had, typically, overlooked, is that Stresa happens to be in Italy, while Locarno is in Switzerland. The result was that on the first day of the conference an entire boatload of delegates set off from Stresa for Locarno but without thinking to bring along their passports. In consequence they were not allowed to land on Swiss soil and were advised to sit on the boat all the way back to Stresa. But this was by no means the end of their torment. Arriving in Stresa, they were again denied landing rights, this time for having come from the neighbouring country, Switzerland, without a passport. Suddenly their ultimate destiny impressed itself on their horrified vision – that of spending the whole of the rest of one's life on a motorboat going indefinitely between Stresa and Locarno and back. Needless to say it was the Italians who

13

ultimately took pity on them and all they had missed was a few tiresome welcoming introductory speeches.

I am glad to say that, over the years, Geneva's level of helpless incompetence, unlike the bogus, glossy glamour of the organization in New York, has simply been updated. In 1936, on the day of Hitler's invasion of the Rhineland – the first of the series of aggressions which led to World War II – the Palais was in session. The subject: a ninety-four nation conference on the standardization of level-crossing signs throughout the world . . . .

Today we have advanced. Last time I was at the Palais it was a 142-nation conference on the standardization of container traffic. In this, the larger states, such as Britain and France, had brought delegations involving seventy or eighty experts; while it is, of course, common for the Superpowers, say the US or Russia, to field delegations involving hundreds or even thousands of experts. Would you like to see all of this in action? What you do is put on a suit, go in after lunch and look official. If stopped and your accreditation demanded, produce any official-looking document (I usually use a Sketchley laundry ticket), then stride purposefully up to any desk labelled 'non-governmental delegates', sit down and put on the earphones – you're in for a treat.

You may notice instantly that there is an astonishingly high proportion of attractive young women among the delegates, but before you start lamenting that such beauty should be wasted in a wilderness of container traffic, be reassured! It is simple. Following their gigantic expenses-paid lunch, most of the delegates have gone to use up some more of their expenses gambling in the Casino at Divonne. Having arrived at Divonne, they suddenly remember the conference and ring up their embassies with a request that secretaries on the embassy staff take their place . . . . Virtually the only genuine delegate who had made the container traffic conference session at the same time as myself was an enormous African from Chad. Unlike the secretaries, he seemed to have at least some vague idea which way his government intended

14

to vote. Imagine my horror then when, after he had sat down, the president, looking directly at me, asked me what was my view as the only representative of the American government at present in the chamber. Well, in Geneva, illusions are too precious to be destroyed. I tried to behave as I am sure the American delegate would have done – that is to say I complained on a point of order, to whit that the French spoken by the honourable delegate from Chad was quite incomprehensible and that my government would therefore greatly prefer classification in writing. How wonderful to have done at least a little something for American diplomacy.

Manoeuvres, military and otherwise

It is, of course, true that a great many disasters have been caused by futile travelling for military purposes, but here comedy is usually, alas, outweighed by tragedy. Not always, however. Take the Fashoda incident of 1881. You don't recall it? Yet for years it was a bitter *cause célèbre* in the struggle between English and French imperialism. It occurred during British involvement in the Sudan in one of Mr Gladstone's more chauvinistic periods as premier. The British became fed up with the fact that the French controlled most of southern Sudan. It was decided to send out an expeditionary force to teach the Frogs a lesson. Since the arrival of this force had to be kept secret, landing in Egypt was out of the question. They therefore landed in West Africa and achieved an amazing 1000-mile march across the continent, pulling two enormous cannons.

When they arrived at the French position, they were distressed to find this very strongly fortified and that they were outnumbered by at least ten to one. The French commander, Marchant, on noticing the arrival of this, presumably enemy, force, sent them a polite note asking them if they would like to surrender or fight some kind of token battle. (One recalls the elegance of the French request to the

15

'. . . they even watched with complete indifference as my terrified friend
jumped out of the carriage . . .'

British at the Battle of Fontenay, where the two opposing sides, groups of officers rather, met in the middle of the field, the British enquiring, 'Should we fire first, or would you like to?' and the French officers replying, *'Messieurs les anglais, tirez vous les premiers.'*)

Over an excellent dinner, it was agreed that the British should depart the following morning, after firing a couple of token cannon shots at some militarily insignificant part of the fortifications. They did so, and made another epic journey back, to receive in London a welcome not unworthy of that accorded to Wellington's army after Waterloo – despite the fact that no one had ever heard of Fashoda or had the slightest idea if it had any importance or not. Marchant's gentlemanliness was not mentioned; what mattered was that the French had been punished for daring to raise the tricolour on the banks of the Nile.

Since that distant epoch, the helpless incompetence of military strategy involving travel has not changed, despite modern techniques of communication. It has merely been updated. An example to ponder is that of the Chaco War of 1929–32, the last important conflict between South American mainland states, in this case Bolivia and Paraguay. Unlike the Fashoda incident, this was a sanguinary conflict with a great many casualties; its relevance to our theme is, however, that all these were caused purely by travel.

The two sides virtually never engaged at all. The Bolivians began by sending their unfortunate army down from on high into the fever-ridden swamps of Paraguay where, of course, most of the troops died of every tropical disease known to man. The Paraguayans, missing the Bolivian army altogether, then struggled up into the Andes, where they were equally struck down by the wide range of illnesses you get if you start force-marching at 10,000 feet having lived all your life at sea level. In fact, the wretched remnants of the forces involved made virtually no contact at all for three years, by which time they were so decimated that the entire war had to be decided by arbitration.

The Chaco War is an excellent example of the fact that South Americans live on the whole in a state of splendid insularity, unaware of the most basic conditions in neighbouring states, let alone of anything that may be going on in North America or Europe. They simply have the good sense not to travel, perhaps because, as that doyen of travel writers Peter Fleming shows us (*Brazilian Adventure*), South American travel is far too unpleasant to appeal to any but an insane masochist (and South Americans are very far from that); perhaps also because for centuries the government of the Spanish Empire, with untypical intelligence, forbade its component parts to trade with each other – everything had to be done through Madrid. (Vestiges of this attitude are still to be found, except that Madrid has, of course, given way to more powerful forces. Any major bank in Brazil, for instance, would today route a call to its *own* branch in Lima or Montevideo via New York!) It was this approach which also turned the efforts of both British and German military missions in Latin America at the beginning of World War II into one long travel disaster of the most farcical kind.

The object was to persuade each state to enter the conflict on one's own side or, failing that, to maintain a benevolent neutrality or, failing even that, at least not join the enemy's side. Needless to say, the delegates found themselves staying in the same hotel in every single capital. Yet more embarrassing than the frozen silence of the breakfast room was that when they got to work, they both found themselves talking to a high proportion of people who were completely unaware that a world war had broken out at all, let alone who the conflicting parties might be. (I can well imagine this – in São Paulo, Brazil, 1977, I met an elderly Italian lady who was not only unaware of the Second World War but even of the First. At one point she enquired after the health of the King of Italy.)

Ultimately both British and Germans returned in despair. Sir Roland Barton of the Foreign Office recalls as his only personal achievement on this occasion the avoidance of some

'. . . the six passengers tried waving and shouting "shoo" . . .'

dreadful incident when he managed to persuade an ultra pro-British barber in Lima not to cut the throat of the next customer – the head of the German delegation. Anyway, who's to say diplomacy never bears fruit . . . Peru did ultimately swing its whole armed might behind the Allies – in April 1944!

Manoeuvres of Amazonian proportion

Which brings us to more modern times still, and a travel disaster so immense as to be unique in history so far. This is the creation of the Trans-Amazonic highway which will, when complete, link the Brazilian coast with the Peruvian border – a distance of over 4500 miles. I hope I won't offend my South American friends if I say that the fantastic notion of cutting a super-highway, longer than the journey from Lisbon to Moscow, through impenetrable jungle, along the very course of the longest navigable river on earth, could only have occurred to a Brazilian. But I mention it in this context because it is in fact a military travelling disaster rather than a means of transportation; car ownership tends to be rather limited in a country seventy per cent of whose inhabitants are outside the money economy altogether . . . .

The insane decision to build it was taken in 1967 as a result of a *Time* magazine article in which an American general was misquoted as implying that it might be a great idea for the USA to annex the whole of northern Brazil, what with all those minerals, potential oil fields, the political instability, inflation, and so forth. The Brazilian government thereupon decided that a vast road might somehow validate its territorial claim to the area. It's not easy to get people to work on it. Quite apart from the appalling natural hazards, there are the Indians, whose attitude is, to put it mildly, hostile. (I fear they might not be too helpful when, in due course, family cars start breaking down halfway along the route.) One group of workmen digging the road accidentally left their

'. . . Come here, Mary . . .'

transistor radio on all night. In the morning they found it riddled with poisoned arrows – the Indians had thought it was a hostile god. How true, and how very profound of them. Just so must the Aztecs have watched Stout Cortez land in Mexico on Good Friday, bearing aloft the image of the new god come, unwittingly, to destroy them.

Transport . . . To Paradise

Which mode of travel, one wonders, is the most alarming, the most conducive to disaster? I suggest they are all equally appalling.

Trains and planes

Will you go by train as opposed to air? Then you should remember that, in an event pregnant with symbolism, the very first train ever to run immediately struck down and killed the Minister Huskisson, who had just opened the railway line from Stockton to Darlington and sent the train on its first journey. Furthermore, trains often arrive at the wrong destination. They split up, leaving one in the wrong part. I bade a cheerful farewell to a girlfriend in Milan; she hoped to wake up in Calais and couldn't understand it when her passport was demanded at the East German frontier. Misdirecting trains is, however, normally a specifically Italian pastime. You can still see in Rome's station Mussolini's special train, a gleaming Fascist spaceship capable of travelling from Rome to Milan in under four hours, with all the lines cleared. Few realize, however, that when in 1923 the dictator was refused admission to La Scala by Toscanini for the first performance of *Turandot*, his humiliation had already begun. On the arrival of his train in Milan, an anti-Fascist signalman directed it into a remote marshalling yard and blocked it in with a goods train. The infuriated *Duce* had to walk half a mile over the tracks back to the station, getting his beautiful boots all dirty.

For all that, the Italian railway system is surely still the most splendid in the world. You could probably even now hire the *Duce*'s splendid train if you asked for it; or, if not content with that, peruse the small print at the back of the Italian railway guide. How about a *salone viaggante?* This is no mere railway carriage but – as the name implies – a drawing room on wheels which will convey you and up to twenty friends anywhere you like, from Sicily to the Alps, in – I quote – 'stately comfort'. It can be hitched on to the back of any other train in the scheduled service and you will have scant problem in reaching your destination on time since its mere presence on any train – even the humblest *rapido*, undoubtedly the slowest of the lot – gives that train absolute priority. Thus the Rome–Paris express will grind to a halt as you chug past, enjoying the *servizio splendido* which is thrown in, not to mention the charming *brani musicali* (musical passages – Vivaldi *et al.*) which go so well with the landscape. Of course, if you can't run to an entire *salone viaggante*, there is always a *salotto viaggante* (twelve people) or even the humble *salottino viaggante* (six) – a mere one and a half times the normal first-class fare.

All very well, you think, to find these in the Italian Bradshaw. But does anybody ever use them? Indeed they do – this may well, in fact, account for at least some of the inexplicable delays, changes of direction and so forth, which are so vital a feature of Italian rail travel. I can, however, only describe one disaster known to me directly attributable to their use. In this an art historian, so eminent that for once he must be nameless, was invited to a conference in Bergamo, in the Alps, northeast of Milan. He was engaged in intensive research in Rome and declined the invitation. Ever more desperate pleas arrived, culminating in the sort of offer you presumably can't refuse – especially if you're a foreign art historian with a side interest in prehistoric railway systems. It was no less than this. A *salone viaggante* would be placed at his disposal at Rome station, full *servizio* laid on (I believe there's a special *salotto refrigerato* for the Asti Spumante or do I

24

exaggerate?) and, of course, he could bring along as many friends as he wished – up to twenty, of course, though perhaps the *dottore* would prefer to bring no more than one? Naturally he relented. They set out and the journey was delightful, the *servizio* perfect. They made high speed to Florence, then decoupled from the express and joined the milk train for Perugia in order to get a glimpse of Lake Trasimene at dawn. In fact there were no disasters at all until – like the *Duce* – the moment of their arrival. It was then that they found that the station guard had forgotten that the doors of a *salone viaggante* are self-locking. They couldn't get out! There they sat in the *salone,* in intolerable luxury, the wretched *brani musicali* unswitchoffable, drowning their cries for help. They had – how can I relate it? – to smash their way out of their prison with a case full of empty Asti Spumante bottles and, like the *Duce,* tread a weary way from their remote siding to Platform One . . . .

I may add that getting locked in trains used also to be, in the world of lower than Sotheby's/Christie's-level antique dealers, not so much an occasional disaster as an occupation-al hazard. In the infinitely remote epoch when sales were occasionally 'ringed' – a shocking malpractice, now of course defunct, by which a group of dealers would collude to offer the seller an artificially low price and then re-auction the object among themselves – one of the main dangers was that the news of the 'ring's' intervention would leak out. In a trice dozens, perhaps hundreds, of London-based dealers would become suddenly acutely interested in an obscure country sale. All would get on the only train likely to be available, arriving somewhere near their destination – in remotest Norfolk, for instance, after several changes – only to find that a local rival had *bribed the guards* to lock all the carriages. The train would then sweep on to, say, Overly Staithe, where its desperate passengers would fight their way out, only to find that every taxi within fifty miles of the area had been mysteriously engaged that very morning, for the whole day.

I have never been in a train accident myself. Apparently

25

they have the great advantage that you can feel them coming. A dozen people got out of the train before the great Tay Bridge disaster. They stood huddled together in the night on the platform of the tiny Scottish station, the last before the bridge, unable to explain why they had left the train, except that they had had an imperative urge to do so.

A rather more obvious premonition occurred to a friend of mine travelling on the Indian railways. Despite the trance-like state induced by a vast journey over the sub-continent, he suddenly began to feel that he had seen this particular bit of country before, recently. A quick check revealed that this was true, but that it was only his own carriage, the last, which had become decoupled and was going backwards, rolling down an ever steeper gradient. Reference had been made at the last station to another train, following on the same line. My friend dashed from one group of passengers to another, frantically explaining their predicament: that a collision was inevitable. No effect at all. The Amritsar housewives continued their chatter, the two Bengali businessmen their game of chess. They even watched with complete indifference as my terrified friend jumped out of the carriage into a paddy field. He watched the train disappear; never heard of it again.

Wrong direction: that is so often the key, especially in disasters involving flights. At least trains stay, hopefully, on the rails, but aircraft wander about all over the sky. Take One-Way Corrigan, for instance, the great American pilot of the twenties, whose sense of direction was such that on one occasion he flew the entire Atlantic by mistake, at night, and on seeing the rolling Irish hills at dawn was convinced that he had at last reached up-state Vermont.

As for more ordinary flying accidents, I find it significant that almost everyone I know has had one. A few, however, have borne the experience with the aplomb of the journalist Mark Amory, the only passenger crash-landing in a Cessna in the middle of the Castilian plain. He was absolutely immersed in the *amour de Swann* passage in Proust when the pilot suddenly said, 'Mark, I'm afraid we're coming down!'

'. . . and shot the puppet six times through the head . . .'

Indeed it was true. Death rattles from the engine were followed by a desperate effort to avert a stall. The feeling, as Mark put it, was that of suddenly getting into a New York express lift. What, I asked, did you do? Mark's reply again demonstrated the spirit of the essential traveller. 'Well, since I could do nothing and the end appeared inevitable, I was at least determined to find out how Swann seduces Odette before I died. So I simply concentrated on the novel.' Luckily both men escaped from the crash unscathed, though the plane was a complete write-off and, needless to say, it was the two subsequent weeks of official interviews, explanations and paperwork which constituted the truly miserable part of the disaster.

No less cool under stress was another friend, Jeremy McDonough, whose experience was just as alarming but much more bizarre. Half an hour into a flight up-country in Botswanaland, flying over the deepest jungle, the aircraft was suddenly attacked by a vulture which started taking great bites out of the wing. It had been drawn up to that height by a freak thermal current. The six passengers tried waving and shouting, 'Shoo! Go away!', but it was only when the creature had gnawed its way through most of the right wing and put its head into the cabin to say hallo that the aircraft finally destabilized and crashed in the middle of the jungle. Luckily, the local tribe turned out to be friendly and agreed to conduct the party, all suffering from delayed shock at different moments, on a horrifying twenty-mile trek through waist-deep swamp to the nearest outpost of civiliza-tion, a vast stockaded farm owned by a formidable German lady in the Baroness Blixen mould. Delighted at this unex-pected company, she plied the already groggy party with so much champagne that they were barely able to board the plane. She then radioed another plane to take them on to their next destination which was, of all things, an immensely elaborate dinner party. 'My dears,' said their hostess when they arrived,' you look too, too exhausted. Have you had a particularly trying journey?'

'...SORRY MISTAKE. SKETCHBOOK BLATANT FORGERY...'

Paradise lost

Most dreadful of air disasters known to me, however, is one involving the loss of a blossoming love, of a potential marriage. My friend Timothy was deeply enamoured of a most beautiful but extremely highly-strung Brazilian lady who, after several years and immense difficulties (the case had to be heard in Israeli, French, British and Brazilian courts), had obtained a divorce. She and Timothy celebrated a pre-nuptial honeymoon, tense but delicious, in Rome, flying back to London with Air France. Heathrow was, however, fog-bound. The aircraft returned to Paris and the passengers were forced to stay overnight in that dreadful airport hotel. The food is unspeakable; you can't even get something like the only dish on offer at Boston Airport, a 'Controltower burger' . . . . This particular evening, however, there was no food of any kind and no double room. They went to bed hungry, exhausted and miserable in separate rooms, on separate floors. Nicole was wiping away a tear or two and offered no kiss. Storm warnings – Timothy knew the signs.

Naturally Timothy had left word that they were to be awakened first thing in the morning, well in time to catch the flight on to London. Yet he woke up under his own steam and looked at his watch: 10.30! The plane was about to leave. He rang Nicole's bedroom – no answer. Rushing downstairs he established that indeed they had awakened madame but had forgotten monsieur . . . . He took a taxi to the airport. They were actually boarding the aircraft but the gates were shut. In an agony of rage and despair he saw Nicole, her face a mask of cat-like fury, enter the plane. It took off and he followed in the next one. Poor Timothy. There was no answer from her apartment when he arrived, but there was a note at his own, informing him that the prospect of married life with one who would dump her, unfed, in the worst hotel she had ever known and then not bother to wake up in the morning to take her out of it . . . well, it just wasn't on. Good luck and goodbye. And, indeed, it proved the end. She never re-lented. As a bitter Timothy put it to me, 'Thank you very much, Air France.'

This terrible story, of course, takes the lid off the ludicrous idea that travel and romance somehow go together. Oh no! How many well-tried friendships, burgeoning loves, even devoted marriages has one *not* seen crack under the strain of the final lost suitcase, lost passport, missed connection, surly waiter, insolent hotelier. In deepest confidence my friend Lady Sarah revealed that only once had her marriage nearly come unstuck. On a recent holiday in Ceylon, her husband, a trendy film director who sees the world essentially as a set run by a pretty lousy floor manager, ate something which confined him, moaning and groaning, to bed. Conventional Western medicine having, as usual, no effect, the desperate Sarah enquired around the small township in the south of Ceylon where they were staying. She got results. It turned out that there was a well-known witch doctor resident in a village deep in the jungle not far away. They would be escorted there.

On arrival, the witch doctor studied David with particular care. He got him to recite every detail of his life from the hour of his birth to that moment, though how much of that saga could have been comprehensible to him one could only guess. He then disappeared into some kind of inner sanctum, returning after a considerable time with a small dark bottle. 'Drink this,' he said. 'A few drops every day.' At this point Sarah was overcome by a wave of delightfully feminine jealousy. Why should she have to listen to David's tedious life story and then be faced by the prospect of seeing him down his magic potion day after day while she had nothing? On impulse she asked the witch doctor if he could possibly make her a really good hair conditioner. 'Of course, my dear.' Again he disappears. Again he returns, with a brown glass bottle similar to the first. 'Try that, every other day.' Sarah was in seventh heaven; she could already see Vidal Sassoon's excitement at the mere thought of collaborat-

31

ing with a Ceylonese witch doctor over the problem of her hair . . . .

Back at the hotel, Sarah put the stricken David straight to bed, leaving the bottles on the window sill. Once settled, she poured him a few drops. He didn't seem to like it much but immediately fell into a deep sleep. Sarah couldn't wait. She had a shampoo and applied the conditioner. Feeling pretty drowsy herself, she went to bed as well.

The next morning the situation had changed. David was feeling notably worse. As for Sarah, long blond streaks had started appearing in her lustrous dark hair. The process continued rapidly; by lunchtime she was more blond than dark. It was David who realized it first. 'You bitch, you swapped the bottles around! ' Indeed, an emergency check with the witch doctor proved it. Sarah had been plastering her hair with David's tummy medicine while David had been systematically swallowing Sarah's hair conditioner. The witch doctor provided suitable antidotes but Sarah capped the whole disaster on the final day. As they were packing to go to the airport she dropped David's bottle. It smashed and a vengeful, hysterical David hurled her hair conditioner against the wall. Thus in embittered silence did our two travellers leave the island paradise.

Love on the high seas

Surely, the reader asks, is there not one area where travel and love indisputably meet? The shipboard romance! This crazy notion derives from the fact that people stuffed to the gills with food and drink and feeling distinctly queasy as the 'stabilized' ship rolls in heavy seas simply have a pathetic urge to cling together. The whole concept derives from the early Cook's tour epoch of nineteenth-century travel. A luxury train is created so that one might enjoy it on land, the luxury liner promises that one might do so by sea. The shipboard romance is born. Previously manifestly impossible, it becomes the staple fare of novelists ranging from Barbara Cartland to Evelyn Waugh.

Yet I wonder how many of my readers have ever, in fact, experienced what happened to Ryder in *Brideshead Revisited*, his passion for Julia inside the cabin matched by the storm of the elements outside. In my own experience, this really was a fate worse than death. I was crossing the Atlantic from Rio to Genoa in a dear old Italian boat, the *Giulio Cesare*, in a cabin containing four other men (all I could afford). The very first night there was a dance at which under the starlight I became deeply enamoured of an enchanting Uruguayan girl. The only problem was where to take her, what to do with her? Eventually an idea occurred to me. I would press my suit to her in a lifeboat. Of course I had no idea that a modern lifeboat is a purely practical device; everything in it is sharp and angular. It is very difficult to sit down, let alone to lie down. It is also pitch dark and, once in, it is extremely difficult to clamber out, especially down a thirty-foot ladder wearing a ball gown. But the element which made it so much more frightful than the usual romantic disaster was not the very accurate slap I got for my pains – though that was quite normal and well deserved – it was the fact that I had to spend the whole of the rest of the two-week voyage avoiding the infuriated lady.

To tell you the truth, it was only two years later, far too late, that I discovered that the answer to this problem is to approach one of the junior officers, press 10,000 lire upon him and suggest that he might find an awful lot to do on the bridge rather than in his cabin between, say, midnight and 2.00 a.m . . . .

'Hello, Again.
Remember Me . . . ?'

Hell is indeed other people: either the inseparable companion with whom you go travelling and oh so swiftly find quite intolerable; or, yet worse, the dreaded 'friend' who keeps cropping up wherever you go, who seems almost to be shadowing your footsteps. An unrivalled example of this is the extraordinary relationship between my late friend Martyn Coleman, a distinguished long-time resident of Venice, and the legendary Brian Howard, of all his contemporaries of the twenties and thirties the one most mad, bad and dangerous to know – indeed a gypsy, an itinerant. Martyn, on the other hand, although he had lived in several different countries, was in fact the antithesis of the traveller. He put down the most profound roots wherever he went; his knowledge was encyclopaedic (I saw a proof copy of Hugh Honour's superb *Companion Guide to Venice*. It was marked: 'To Martyn, in trepidation').

Traveller meets non-traveller

However, apart from his vast expertise – the expertise of one who stays in his adopted home to some purpose – Martyn, the non-traveller, was an unrivalled observer of travellers, especially Americans. It was he who first explained to me, for instance, the reason for the frequently extraordinary behaviour of American tourists in Italian restaurants. The fact is that they have all been taught that the crucial word, waiter, is the unpronounceable *cameriere*. To surmount this, the traditional American method is, apparently, to shout the words, 'Come here, Mary', slurring them together as much as possible. This explains why you occasionally see a baffled American paterfamilias shouting, 'Come here, Annie, or was it Jennie?' 'No, honey, it's Mary.' 'Oh, that's it, come here, Mary!' '*Si, signore* . . . .'

Again, it was typically Martyn who overheard, on a plane coming in to land at Venice, a couple from Dallas, or possibly Fort Worth, say, 'My God, what a place to build a city.' But at least they knew roughly where they were, if not quite what to expect. Here from Martyn's treasure trove of anecdotes is another example of geographical dislocation, truly worthy of One-Way Corrigan. A complete American family, who had heard of Venice only as Venice-Lido, arrived at Venice airport, asked for Venice-Lido and were therefore put on a motorboat and taken straight there. For two weeks they resided in one of those awful, seedy, second-rate hotels whose remote heyday was so beautifully portrayed in Visconti's film, *Death in Venice.* All this time, these people actually believed that the Lido, that miserable, overpriced mudbank, was in fact Venice itself. Then, one day, their youngest son arrived late for lunch. 'Mom,' he said, 'I'm sorry I'm late but I've been exploring. I've found another island, near Venice, but quite different. It's much bigger than Venice and it's got churches, palaces, a whole lot of canals and a great big square . . . .'

I was aware that, apart from his masterly observation of the travelling fraternity, Martyn had met, or at least rubbed shoulders with, some of the best-known travellers of his time: Paddy Leigh-Fermor, Xan Fielding, Ian Fleming and, it suddenly occurred to me, why not Brian Howard? This rang an immediate bell, though I couldn't at first think what the fastidious, urbane Martyn could have in common with the crazed, flamboyantly baroque Howard. In fact, the fantastic story surpassed my wildest expectations. This, at its most desperately extreme, is what happens when traveller and non-traveller meet.

'. . . when he managed to persuade an ultra pro-British barber in Lima not actually to cut the throat of the next customer – the head of the German delegation . . .'

It began inauspiciously in a Paris nightclub, circa 1931. A mutual Oxford friend introduced Martyn, whereupon Howard, who was under the influence of heaven-knows-what, grossly insulted him. That's one person, thought Martyn, as he returned to his house in Asolo near Venice, whom, thank goodness, I'll never see again. How wrong he was! A few days later, he received a deeply worried telephone call from the local police chief. They were holding a man called Howard, caught making somewhat questionable approaches to a choirboy actually *in* the cathedral. 'He describes himself as a close friend of yours.' Could Martyn come at once to help sort out the situation . . . . Repressing his indignation, Martyn sped to the scene and dealt manfully with the bishop, the *carabinieri*, the choirmaster, assorted newspaper men, etc. The charges were dropped in exchange for a promise from Howard to leave the area at once and behave himself in the future. In a nutshell, to go away. But that's not how it is with travellers, they don't just go away – that would in almost every case be ideal. They tend to return.

Who needs friends . . . ?

To bring you, dear reader, back to the startling figure of Brian Howard. I should explain that he is the original of Anthony Blanche, now familiar to all through that rather heavy-handed TV adaptation of *Brideshead Revisited*. One of the great wits of Oxford of the early twenties, along with Evelyn Waugh, John Sutro and Harold Acton. Instead of hanging around, however, he went travelling, and his next appearance in my friend Martyn's life was even more alarming.

Another telephone call, this time not from Asolo but from Venice and, even more alarmingly, from Harry's Bar. Arrigo Cipriani in person. 'Dear Mr Coleman, we've got this fellow in here who is a close friend of yours.' 'Really, who?' 'Well, he's called Mr Howard.' 'Oh no, what has he done now?' 'Well, he has just stabbed a negro friend of his with a fork.

There's a certain amount of blood around the place plus, of course, a large number of very worried *carabinieri* and ambulancemen, and it's not really very good for business. Could you possibly come and sort it out?'

Martyn dutifully arrives at Harry's Bar to find a scene which would not have disgraced the most stupendous days of Hemingway, another great traveller, who, according to Cipriani, still owes Harry's Bar an estimated two and a half million lire for sandwiches and Bellini alone . . . . Bellini, in case you didn't know, is a wonderful mixture of peach juice and champagne, carefully laced with a certain amount of vodka. It is the sort of experience which tends to terminate your travel. After five or six Bellinis you feel as if you have travelled an immense distance, even though you haven't moved an inch from Harry's Bar. Yet the travelling thing somehow persists. An American lady sitting opposite me last time I was there simply got up, slapped me on the back and left me with the words, 'Hope to see you in Acapulco next year.' Forgive me, we digress. Brian Howard's travels, accordingly, were by no means yet at an end.

Shaken by the Harry's Bar incident, Martyn decided to drive straight down the peninsula, in fact as far away from northern Italy as possible. He, I hasten to add, was a competent driver who had a real driving licence. He was not reduced, like a friend of mine, to the constant use of a Sketchley laundry ticket in lieu of any official document. (This is the sort of detail that always turns out to be vital when travelling.)

Martyn, again like certain well-known travellers, thought of this journey as a form of escape. Let us accompany him in spirit as he arrives in the remote Gargano peninsula. Here he found an incredibly small and remote hotel. Yet just as he drove up to the door, he noticed an enormous Rolls Royce sitting in the drive. In a desperate double-take, worthy of all the greatest early silent films put together, he grasped that it was Howard's car and tried to turn round. Too late. Pursuing him was the familiar chanting, yet desperately urgent voice,

'Martyn, how wonderful to see you. I didn't expect you here!'

Well, what can one say? Obliged to turn back, Martyn joined Howard for dinner. This went all right; in fact it wasn't until 2.00 a.m. that the next Howard disaster broke out. This time it was truly terrible – the entire hotel was on fire. Howard had given up merely stabbing his friend with a fork and had decided to set fire to the bed instead. The result was an even more startling combination of police, troops, *carabinieri*, firemen, priests, etc., than ever before. Once again Martyn poured as much oil as he could on the troubled waters and continued his flight to the south.

Anxious to put some kind of really serious geographical barrier between himself and Howard, he caught the night ferry from Naples to Palermo. The boat sank! I know you won't believe this but it really happened. Fortunately, it wasn't very far from Palermo and all aboard made it safely to the shore. Martyn, now totally unnerved by this latest catastrophe, decided he could use a few days' rest in Taormina. He hired a car and drove across Sicily. (God knows how – it wasn't until 1983 that the Italian government finally completed the Palermo–Messina motorway originally begun by Mussolini's engineers in 1936.) Anyway, by this time his entire life had become dedicated to one single object: safety from Howard. Other dangers and difficulties were of little, if any, consequence; the fact, for example, that he, a comparatively wealthy individual, was driving in a large car, alone and unescorted through Sicily's most notorious bandit country at the height of the reign of the great bandit, Salvatore Giuliano. Indeed, being captured and held to ransome by Salvatore was just about the only travelling disaster that didn't befall Martyn on this particular trip. I may add that in this period large numbers of American ladies made this same journey *in the hope* that this would happen and that they *would* be captured by Giuliano, preferably with interesting acts of personal violence thrown in . . . .

Well, just as Martyn, having got through that one, was relaxing in one of Taormina's nicest bars (this is before

Taormina became totally ruined by tourism and travel) whom should he see approaching? Yes, you've guessed. However, this time, the story, unlike most travelling disasters, ends in a definite climax. As Howard reached the door, a really firm, middle-aged American lady put her arm across it and barred it with the epic words, 'I think someone round here ought to give this guy the bum's rush.' Howard stalked off, head held high, and that was the last anyone ever saw of him.

Puppets and poets . . . .

Having mentally accompanied Martyn to Sicily, let us linger a little in this most beautiful of islands. Time in Sicily stands absolutely still. When I visited the Villa Palagonia, just outside Palermo, complete with its wonderful orchestra of stone monkeys, the incredible aged lady who looks after the place kept referring to the great poet who was there. 'When was he here?' I enquired. 'Oh, quite recently.' Well, I naturally assumed she meant at least in her lifetime. 'He was a foreign poet.' How interesting. D H Lawrence or Baron Corvo perhaps? But further questioning elicited the fact that she could remember that he was *un poeta tedesco,* a German poet. My goodness, whom could she be referring to? There are some distinguished poems on Sicily by Heinrich Böll. Maybe it was him, perhaps even Rilke? But no, eventually the truth emerged. Incredibly she was referring to the visit of Goethe in 1772 and he, of course, ran slap bang into the same disasters as I did.

The villa Palagonia was built in 1750 by a really manic eccentric count with an enthusiasm for playing practical jokes on his guests. These all took the most childish form. For example, every chair in the drawing room either collapses when you sit on it or throws you up to the ceiling or, like the one I, and Goethe before me, sat on, sends a jet of intensely cold water up your posterior. Just my luck to choose that one. But though it was a travelling disaster, it is nice to know that one has something in common with Goethe, if only that . . . .

40

'. . . the Indians had thought it was a hostile god . . .'

In fact, water plays a big part in Sicilian travel disasters. The very day after this, I visited the great Greek temple at Segesta. There is only one local hotel to stay in, an appalling, rotten construction, obviously put up by the local mafia with the aid of some crooked grant from the Sicilian tourist board. My night was disturbed by weird groaning and moaning noises, which I first assumed to be merely typical, like, say, the local mafia hanging some unfortunate farmer from the nearest tree. But it wasn't until I woke up in the morning to find my bed floating in water four feet deep that I realized that it was only the plumbing. I hardly expected in the middle of Sicily in high summer to have to swim for my life but at least I didn't actually drown.

Returning to Palermo, I was again confronted by another disaster. This time it was my dear friend, Ferrucio, who is the finest puppet master on the island. Now, I don't know how much you know about the traditional puppet theatre in Sicily. The main theme is the Crusades, starring a good knight called Rinaldo and an absolutely awful villain called Gano, a worse-than-Judas who betrays the Christian knights to the Infidels. When Gano appears, the audience normally pelts him with eggs, old beer bottles or anything else that comes to hand. But this time, on a provincial tour, things were different – and worse. A member of the audience became so incensed by Gano's activities that he got up and shot the puppet six times through the head, luckily just missing Ferrucio, who was hiding in the wings. The only upshot of the incident was, therefore, the loss of a very valuable Sicilian puppet – this one was late eighteenth century and you couldn't buy one today for less than five hundred pounds. As Ferrucio said, 'I'm never, never going travelling again.' I may add that, even in Palermo, odd things do occasionally happen with the puppets. On one occasion a man bought a Gano for five hundred pounds, took it out in a boat from Marsala harbour and drowned it.

I looked in vain for one who could match the Coleman/ Howard saga of the unwanted friend. But in the end I am

'... James arrived dressed as death ...'

forced to admit that one of my own experiences is, once again, the worst. Having resolved to spend upwards of a year in Venice, I had the extraordinary luck to be offered an enormous flat in an eighteenth-century palace in Castello, a very non-touristy old quarter near the park where they hold the Biennale. The owner, the poet Peter Russell, a pupil and friend of Ezra Pound, had been invited to become poet-in-residence at one of those American liberal arts colleges whose distance from Boston, as Scott Fitzgerald puts it, has only ever been measured in the time it takes a Rolls Royce to make the journey.

The first day was delicious. I simply could not take in that I now had my own flat in Venice. I sat on the roof at sunset, watching the great ships berthing at the end of the Riva, listening, I remember, to the Brahms cello sonatas. Naturally, all this didn't last long. The very next day, at the same witching hour, the bell rang and I was confronted by a tall, rangey black American. 'Is Peter in?' 'No, I'm afraid he's in America.' 'Like, man, like we're the Living Theatre, man, like we always stay here, man.' Well, I felt it would be churlish to break with Peter's tradition of hospitality to a small, worthy group of actors but I confess I was stunned when some thirty marijuana-puffing, Damon Runyon characters came pouring round the corner into the flat.

The first night's party stamped pretty firmly on my elegant recluse/*Death in Venice* vision. I was not surprised when I was summoned to the office of the Chief of Police the next day. Apparently the Living Theatre's hijinks had disturbed neighbours as far away as the Rialto. I was, of course, responsible. Were these, the Commissario wanted to know, typical of my friends? 'No, no, Signor Commissario, I never saw them before in my life.' 'What? You admitted these appalling characters to your flat without ever having seen them before in your life? Yet my officers report that there was evidence in your flat this morning of a consumption of illegal substances. Do you not realize that this could be the basis of serious charges? Have a care, Dottore Vickers, we have an old

Venetian saying, *"Le bugie vanno sulle gambe corte."* – "Lies go on short legs".' At which, for once in my travels, a flash of inspiration arrived to help me out of a tight corner. 'I can but reply to you, *Signor Commissario,* in the words of another Venetian proverb, *"Non dico mai bugie, ma la verità non a tutti."* – "Do not tell lies, but the truth not to everyone".' The Commissario burst into delighted laughter. I had clearly passed some sort of traveller's test. The next day the Living Theatre was given a massive police escort and taken to the Austrian border to be let loose on Salzburg and Vienna. My own flat remained ravaged but intact . . . .

A little later, I realized that Peter had left me not only a flat but an entire profession. This was 'coaching' delightful girls who attended the Ca' Foscari University in Venice for their English Studies. The climax, without which no degree could be obtained, was a thesis on some aspect of English literature. Here Peter's mantle fell full upon me. He would write everybody's thesis for a certain sum, not, I gathered, payable in cash in every case. In his absence I found myself frantically recalling all I knew of pre-Elizabethan lyric poets, John Donne's sermons, French influences on the *Rape of the Lock,* post-Freudian interpretations of *Wuthering Heights* – in fact the whole dubious intellectual *mélange* collectively known as Eng. Lit.

Yet in the very first week I encountered a crisis. A tearful girl stood on my doorstep. Her thesis, entirely written by Peter, had unprecedentedly been rejected. Its title was 'Byron and Shelley: the Flesh and the Spirit'. I realized at once that Peter had allowed his intense dislike of Byron to surface. Before sitting down to rewrite it myself, I thought it might be as well to ring up the Professor of English Literature in the university to see if a few tips might be forthcoming. How fortunate that I did so. On establishing that my protégé had been coached by Peter, he asked if the distinguished *professore* had in any way helped her with her thesis. 'Why, yes,' I blurted out in a mad fit of honesty, 'he wrote the whole thing.'

This stupefying revelation had quite the opposite effect to that which one would imagine. The embarrassed professor, far from denouncing this scandalous academic fraud, at once replied, 'But I had no idea. My deepest apologies. Please tell Professor Russell that I will immediately upgrade the young lady's marks to alpha-plus . . . .'

A musical note

Now, dear reader, after a last, lingering look at Venice, let us catch an imaginary plane, and with it we will fly north to Vienna. Assuming that we don't dive into the sea or crash into the Gröss Glockner, we might just possibly get there. Tired, shaken and hungry, we will drag ourselves to that excellent, inexpensive, Yugoslav restaurant, The Yadran. But this was the scene of one of the worst travelling disasters of my life. It terminated my employment on one of the very few occasions when I have ever managed to get a job. There I was, sitting with my boss, the head of the classical music section of a certain well-known recording company. Suddenly a brilliant gypsy violinist appeared at our table. My host's dreadful, horse-like face assumed a look presumably intended to suggest agonized distaste.

'He's playing out of tune! ' 'Of course,' I replied, 'that, didn't you know, is a vital part of Hungarian traditional fiddle technique.' But then, suddenly losing my cool altogether, 'How could you possibly know whether he was playing in tune or not? Your only musical background is that you are reputed to have been simply the worst organ scholar in the entire history of King's College, Cambridge.'

Well, I'm afraid that was that. He gave me my marching orders on the spot. But it does delight me to say that he may subsequently have regretted this act, in that just before leaving I was able to complete the production of a recording by the Vienna Octet, which was later hailed by Desmond Shaw-Taylor in *The Sunday Times* as Chamber Music Record of the Year.

The earth moved

As soon as I got back, I received a telephone call from a friend in California, describing that ultimate in travel horrors: an earthquake. I have never been in an earthquake but my friend, Joe Wynn-Linton, an extremely eccentric Irishman, achieved the astonishing feat of going through an entire earthquake without even noticing it. Joe, who is incidentally a piano tuner, was sitting watching TV, having imbibed a considerable quantity of gin, when he suddenly noticed that his glass, which he had at that moment put down on top of the TV set, was shaking violently and the gin was beginning to spill out of it. Naturally, he put this down to some terrible attack of DTs. He was therefore amazed when the television programme was interrupted and an announcer came on saying there had just been a major earthquake in the San Diego area, 7.4 on the Richter scale. 'There may be a second tremor. You are advised to go out immediately. Do not panic.' Joe went out; there was no second tremor but in his condition he was not certain – is not certain even now – whether this whole incident might not be simply part of one of those vast earthquake disaster movies.

Joe himself is a traveller who not merely suffers from, but usually creates, disaster wherever he goes. Staying with me in Milan, for instance, he completely ruined three of Ricordi's finest pianos. At one point he unscrewed the lid of a first-rate Bechstein in order to get at the strings. At this, the whole lid fell off. We had to leave at high speed under the astonished gaze of the chairman of Ricordi's and most of his more important minions. Joe then disappeared completely for two days, reappearing at midnight guarded by two large, armed policemen.

'What has he done now?' I asked. 'Well, we found him stuck on top of the roof of Milan station, having climbed about eighty feet up the wall in order to plant an Irish flag on the top. We had to get the fire brigade to get him down. He

'... and boarding a craft, at night, as unstable as a gondola is not particularly easy ...'

says you are a great friend of his. Can you promise you'll prevent him doing anything like this again?' 'No,' I said, 'I can't promise but I will try.' They left, but as they went the tougher of the two looked at me searchingly and said, 'You give me your word that he didn't do this for political reasons?' 'Oh, absolutely not. Pure *joie de vivre*. You don't know the Irish – they are always like this.' 'OK, maestro, you do your best.'

Travellers' Tales

Those reminiscences of Joe Wynn-Linton in the last chapter suggest to me that I might introduce to the reader a whole *galère* of travellers known to me, some fortunate, others less so, but all familiar with disaster in countless forms.

One castle too many

I should introduce first my friend Robin de La Lanne Mirrlees, former Rouge Dragon Pursuivant at the Royal College of Arms. Robin is one who is by no means short of his fair share of this world's goods, but in about 1970 he began to feel that these didn't include sufficient castles, though he already had an admirable pair of them, one in the western isles of Scotland, the other just outside Cadiz. On a brief trip to Sicily he saw a superb, probably Norman, castle in the extreme southwest corner of the island, loved it and bought it on the spot. I assure the reader that I would not have credited the following sequence of events had I not by chance met in Palermo the lawyer who acted for my friend in the purchase of the castle. The entire transaction had gone through, the money been paid, the insurance work not completed, when the following week there occurred the terrible earthquake of 1969 in southwestern Sicily. Believe it or not, my friend's castle had, luckily, no one in it at the time but it was, on the other hand, the exact epicentre of the earthquake. The whole place was simply a heap of rubble. By the time Robin turned up, there was not one stone standing on another.

The insurance was not complete, nothing could be done. Well, really, I personally didn't shed too many tears of grief. Two castles and three houses, I feel, ought to be sufficient for the simple needs of any bachelor, especially when his main activity is simply sitting at home designing coats of arms . . . .

Return ticket

May I turn now to another traveller known to me: one who, I do believe, would probably have described his essential motivation as simply to go away. This is my friend Nicholas Ward-Jackson, former Director of West European Art, Sotheby's, London, later chairman of Sotheby Parke Bernet, New York. When I was a fellow student with him at the Courtauld Institute, he was spotted by the powers of Bond Street as not merely the most able young art historian of his generation but probably the only one with enough business sense to reckon up a bill, let alone write a cheque. It was, however, when Nicholas won the scholarship to the British Institute in Rome that the approaches of Sotheby's became truly dramatic. Telegram after telegram would arrive: COME BACK AT ONCE STOP NAME YOUR OWN PRICE STOP ASSUME DUTIES TOMORROW.

These Nicholas disregarded, although as his funds, due to his somewhat exaggerated lifestyle, constantly diminished, he began to wonder if Sotheby's might not turn out to be possibly helpful after all. So on the day when his bank account hit the last 200,000 lire, and even the Café Greco in the Via Condolti refused him further credit, he realized that something would have to be done. Now it is at this point that even the master may make an error when, in effect, travelling disasters come into their own. At a country auction near Rome that very afternoon, he discovered a French sketch-book, possibly of the 1820s. Names like Géricault, or conceivably even Delacroix flashed through his mind. He purchased it for 10,000 lire – some five pounds – and sent it off to Sotheby's by urgent post.

He was rewarded by yet another telegram: SKETCHBOOK GENUINE STOP AMAZING DISCOVERY STOP WORTH AT LEAST $100,000 STOP MANY CONGRATULATIONS LOVE SOTHEBY'S. I myself attended the celebratory party which Nicholas organized throughout the following night. To say that the whole of Rome was there would be to do it a grave injustice – rather, the whole of Italy, together with a considerable part of the United States. Indeed, I doubt that since the most tremendous days of the Grand Tour in the eighteenth century has the eternal city witnessed such a spectacular bash.

Few of the guests had gone to bed by the following morning when, needless to say, yet a further telegram arrived from Sotheby's, this time of hideous import: SORRY MISTAKE STOP SKETCHBOOK BLATANT FORGERY STOP TOTALLY WORTHLESS. Whatever do we do now? Nicholas, now millions and millions in debt, was desperately considering the question when, with masterly timing, yet a further telegram appeared. This one read: SUGGEST TAKE ALITALIA AL156 LONDON STOP TICKET WAITING AIRPORT STOP PREPAID TAXI COLLECTS 11.00 STOP LOVE SOTHEBY'S. Thus, brilliantly tricked (if that's the word you like) into accepting the offer, an unwilling Nicholas made his way to London to discover to his amazement that the office designated to him already had a large brass plaque on the door, reading: Nicholas Ward-Jackson, Director, West European Art.

The room contained a desk with seven telephones of assorted colours, but nothing else at all. Uncertain of his duties or compensation, Nicholas sat down at the desk and waited, and waited. None of the telephones rang; in fact nothing happened at all for the first few hours, after which there came a timid knocking at the door. It was four men carrying an enormous Spanish picture which they dumped

'You bloody blundering idiot! What d'you think you're doing?'

against the opposite wall. Invited to offer a few comments on this masterpiece, Nicholas replied, 'But surely it's a copy of a well-known Murillo in the Prado.' 'Brilliant, amazing, what stunning knowledge. But, Mr Ward-Jackson, can you perhaps tell us any more about the copy – the approximate date, for instance?' Nicholas: 'Well, I think it's probably a mid-nineteenth-century German copy.' 'Amazing, how on earth can you tell that?' 'Well, partly on general stylistic grounds but I confess to being somewhat influenced by the fact that if you look carefully at the bottom right-hand corner it does say perfectly clearly "Arnold Schnorr von Bettelsheim, 1849".'

I am delighted to add that after these adventures, our hero triumphantly ended his travels in New York six months later, where he was appointed a Director of Sotheby Parke Bernet at the tender age of thirty.

It's all Greek to me . . . .

Another traveller for whom tragedy and triumph hang on the finest of knife edges is unquestionably the present Earl of Rosse, certainly the most accomplished of all Irish travellers. Brendan Rosse shows an admirably aristocratic disdain for the sort of travel we lesser mortals make; for instance, on his return visits to Ireland he invariably enjoys baffling the Irish customs officials by presenting his UN passport carefully open at the pages which have Russian on the left and Chinese on the right.

Most of the time, however, he works in Morocco as part of an international agricultural advisory committee involving two Americans, one Frenchman, one Italian, one Ethiopian and at least two extremely heavyweight Russians. Now, I ask you to guess which language this heterogeneous body conducts its deliberations in. English, that usual *lingua franca*? On the very first day it emerged that the Russians didn't have a clue about that. What Brendan's masterly chairmanship did establish was that all these people had at one time or another served in Iran. Thus, believe it or not, this impartial international body decides how to come to the aid of Moroccan agriculture in basic *Persian*, though the committee has not one Persian member.

Brendan has, however, made even more remarkable use of his position as a UN official, in this case in relation to his own government. One fine day in Morocco, he received a letter from the Irish government informing him that because he was a full-time paid official of an international government agency, to whit the United Nations, he had forfeited his right to vote in the Irish Republic. Apparently, this sanction is ingrained into the very fabric of the Constitution and cannot be changed. On contacting other Irish friends working for the United Nations in different parts of the world, he was intrigued to discover that all had received the letter from the same imperious little official in Dublin. In due course they managed to get together in Paris to discuss what to do about it. Here Brendan revealed at a stroke the advantages of a trained mind. 'Why don't we remind them,' he suggested, 'of ancient democratic principle? No taxation without representation.' And, indeed, despite the frenzied protests of Dublin, these gentlemen have withheld their taxes ever since – it is now a total of eight years.

Good food and French jails

Now to introduce you to a traveller in many respects very different from Rosse, but similar in that, like him and the other travellers I mentioned, he has been able to use travel disasters to serve a profound personal end. This gentleman is a Frenchman called Jacques Lebrun. His remarkable exploits came to my attention while I was living in Geneva. The local paper, the *Journal de Genève*, reported in tones of shocked horror how, a few days before, Monsieur Lebrun had walked into the best and most expensive restaurant in nearby Grenôble, which is called the Suisse et Bordeaux. He then proceeded to order himself an excellent but tastefully chosen and not-too-lavish meal. He had the local trout, a veal escalope (which the Suisse et Bordeaux does very well), a raspberry sorbet and a couple of local cheeses. He chose the wine with care and even donated a bottle of champagne to the nice Swiss tourists at the next table.

However, when the bill came, a walloping four hundred and twenty-five francs, Jacques simply said, 'I can't pay. Call the police.' Desperate to avoid a scandal, the management told him that they would accept payment in any form, even, say, a postdated cheque, but nothing worked. Jacques refused to budge until the police were eventually called. However, it was his trial the following day which was so sensational. The puzzled magistrate announced that Jacques had committed this same offence in different parts of France on something like 287 previous occasions. He consequently, and most reluctantly in view of Jacques' admirable choice of food and wine, was obliged to hand down a custodial sentence of six months.

Greatly to everyone's astonishment, a smiling Jacques thanked the magistrate profusely, adding, 'Your Honour, your decision will allow me to complete the final section of my masterwork.' 'And what, pray, is that, Monsieur Lebrun?' 'Your Honour, it is a Good Food Guide to French Jails.' I need hardly say that I and a group of fellow students in Geneva formed a Jacques Lebrun fan club, met him out of jail when he emerged after four months (two months' reduction for good behaviour) and, clubbing together our scanty resources, took him straight back to the Suisse et Bordeaux for lunch, which I can only describe as a memorable occasion – in all senses of the word.

Meat, milk and blood

Love, the shipboard romance, erotic emotion on any level – we have agreed that these are entirely incompatible with travelling. But one obscure belief continues to haunt the traveller. This is the fantastic notion that somehow, by dint of travel itself, he is going to find *food* – food, that is to say, seen not as a necessity elevated by decent cooking into a pleasant experience but rather as a mystical goal comparable with that of the pilgrim contemplating the sighs of St Joseph (see *Carnival and Crusades*). How is it then that I have eaten the foulest *gigot d'agneau* in Paris, the most repulsive *ravioli* in Rome, a *paella* in Valencia that even the cat refused? All you have to do is to follow those innumerable trail-breakers – the *Relais Routiers* (have you actually *tried* a meal at one of their restaurants? My God . . .) to the latest Sunday Supplement 'expert' – that is if you really want to wake up at four in the morning, 350 francs the poorer, with an overwhelming uncertainty as to where the *bon patron* said the loo was. No, I am sure I need not expatiate on these experiences, common to us all.

What I would like to add, however, is a note on food in more exotic climes. I have an American friend who teaches in the Open University, all of whose travels have been marked by disasters on a level, for instance, of having to seduce his seventy-year-old landlady in order to get a shower in his first Viennese pension, through to no less than two of his elderly Open University charges dying on him while embarking on a cut-price trip to Florence. (So what? My first cousin, a courier in student days, abandoned all his American charges on a Pyrennean mountain pass in mid-winter. He was rather taken by a gypsy guitarist he had heard in the last village they had passed, so decided to devote some months studying with him.)

To return to food and my Open University friend, Ronald. He was at this point in East Africa and was approached by a member of the Shona tribe who explained that he was desperately hungry. Could Ron possibly help him out? With a typical American generosity, Ron offered him what food he possessed – which happened to be a can of Japanese pilchards. The tribesman couldn't make much sense of this, apparently owing to the fact that Ron had lost his can-opener and all the instructions were in any case in Japanese. One thing however was clear enough. 'Surely,' said the tribesman, 'this can contains fish.' 'Yes,' replied Ron, 'excellent fish. Very good for you, stacked full of protein, highly nutritious . . . . ' 'But Shona-man, him not eat fish.' 'Well,' Ron replies, slightly wounded at so exclusive an attitude in the circumstances, 'what does Shona-man eat?' 'Shona-man him only eat three things. Meat, milk and blood.' 'Well, I'm afraid I haven't actually got any of those, at least in canned form.' So that was that. Shona-man left disappointed but, as Ron so rightly said, 'Supposing it had been the other way round? . . . Had it been us surviving in the desert and Shona-man offered us a nice little bowl of blood and milk?'

Well, it couldn't be any worse than a grouse I had last year at a London restaurant, so famous it must be nameless – a little bag of skin and bone sitting pathetically on a slice of blood-soaked soggy toast – and I didn't even have to travel for that.

It's not who you know . . . .

Let us turn to the world of business for a moment. Consider the saga of David Barhams, now happily playing the stock market from his Scottish fastness, once (incredibly) a trainee product manager in a Dundee bicycle factory. His very successful business career opened out at the moment when his managing director suddenly asked him to meet an important client in London. Golden opportunity! David had never been to London before and was determined to maximize the advantages to be gained from such a vast, unexpected journey.

Somewhere he had heard or read, probably in one of the gossip columns, that Sir Charles Clore invariably lunched at Claridges. On arrival in London, therefore, David telephoned his client and impressed him greatly by suggesting that they themselves lunch at that august establishment. Arriving half an hour early, he was duly rewarded by the sight of Sir Charles ordering a pre-lunch Martini. He followed suit and, taking his courage in both hands, boldly approached the great man. 'Sir Charles, I know that I, a complete stranger, take a great liberty in thus addressing you, but I wondered if I could possibly ask you a small favour?' 'Well, what can I do for you, young man?' 'Sir Charles, I am at the outset of my business career and I'm about to lunch an important client. It would be of immense, inestimable advantage to me if you could possibly, during our lunch, come up to our table and, as it were, pretend to know me . . . . ' 'Well, what impertinence! You ask me this when I've never seen you before in my life? Outrageous.' (*Thinks.*) 'Still, I admire a bit of spirit in a young man . . . must have taken some courage to come up to me like that . . . . Anyway, what do I stand to lose? Well, why not? I'll do it.'

Thrilled by this triumph, David greets his client and they start lunch. No sooner have they begun than Sir Charles enters the dining room, sees their table, gasps with astonishment, sails up to them and slaps David on the back. 'Long time no see, old boy – what are you up to these days? Miss a good second-in-command. Remember when you clinched the Tunisian hospital deal? And the Bahrain city centre contract? Brilliant. Don't know how I get on without you.'

Thus Sir Charles magnificently does his bit. But, alas, it is at this point that David is affected by the fatal hubris of the traveller. It is *because* he made a long journey to achieve this triumph that he now feels insanely invulnerable . . . . 'Look, Charlie,' he replies, 'just go away, would you? Can't you see I'm busy?' Poor young man – Sir Charles simply turns on his heel with the words, 'Of course, David. I only hope your client here won't have to get rid of you as quickly as I did when I started looking through your expense sheets.'

I may add that David himself confided to me that it was the journey which caused this fiasco: the sleepless, ceaseless planning as the train rattled through the night, the sense of unreality on arrival, the headiness of the unexpected triumph. This is indeed the reason why executives are not allowed to take major decisions within twenty-four hours of long international jet flights. On the other hand, it was a salutary lesson for someone of David's intelligence – from then on he became the most stay-at-home person I think I've ever met.

Royal flush

One point in David's favour was that his meeting with Sir Charles did at least have some cogent aim or purpose. What a contrast to an appallingly disastrous journey made by another friend to whom I would like to introduce you in this *galère* of unfortunate travellers – Leo Gardiner. Leo is simply the most snobbish person I've ever met. A founder member of the Monarchist League, his travels consist simply of going anywhere on earth where he might meet and speak to, or even merely gaze at, any person of any royal house, reigning or not. If all else is unobtainable, mere proximity will do. I well remember him queuing to buy a wildly expensive ticket for a charity gala merely in order to sit in the row behind Princess Margaret; and dinners with him invariably involve the same place in the same restaurant merely because Princess Michael of Kent had once sat at the next table.

It was, however, in an earlier pre-war period of his life that the following occurred – a catastrophe which would surely have put off a lesser royalist for life. During the Abdication crisis his sympathies were, of course, entirely with the King – he probably thought that Mrs Simpson would anyway in due course follow Anne Boleyn to Tower Hill. But his sympathies following the Abdication were even more passionately aroused. The Duke, this lonely, exiled wanderer, needed his help. Yes! He needed a friend. At whatever cost, Leo would go and meet him.

His next move surpasses belief. He sold up his flat, his

assets, in fact virtually all his possessions, in order not merely to get to Biarritz where the Duke was currently staying but also to adopt on arrival the kind of lifestyle appropriate to one moving in royal circles. He went to Savile Row and invested in a formidable wardrobe; he also engaged a valet (surely an essential adjunct), booked the largest suite in the Ritz-Carlton and a first-class compartment on the Golden Arrow, then set off from Victoria with a light heart.

All went well at first. He caught constant glimpses of the Duke, sometimes buying something in a shop with Mrs Simpson, sometimes strolling down the Promenade des Anglais – once, sensationally, in the dining room of his own hotel. But how to get closer? No one Leo met seemed to know the Windsors; the hotel concierge assured him that everyone knew the Duke's privacy was sacrosanct; and Leo lacked the courage to approach him himself. After three or four weeks of this tantalizing proximity he became a trifle depressed. He went to see the (by now intensely friendly) hotel manager. 'Monsieur is a little downcast? But I am so sorry to hear it. Perhaps a little visit to the casino? So often, Monsieur, that works wonders,' he purred, thinking of the fat commission he would doubtless soon be receiving from that quarter.

Hesitantly, Leo complied with this advice. An inexperienced gambler, he started with the simplicities of roulette, only to find that within a short time the ancient adage, 'Unlucky in love, lucky at cards', started applying in full force. (For I can assure you, reader, that the word 'love' was entirely appropriate to Leo's feelings for the Duke of Windsor.) It was the game of one's dreams. His every move was successful – a *plein* on nineteen came up three times but Leo didn't even notice because he was concentrating on a complicated and equally successful transversal. An hour into the game an embarrassed croupier was barely able to push Leo his castle-like pile of chips across the baize; the table was surrounded by a fascinated crowd of onlookers some three rows deep.

At this point, just as Leo was setting up a nice little 100,000 franc *cheval,* he noticed an elegant, heavily beringed hand appear over his shoulder, holding a particularly high-denomination chip. 'Glad to see you're clearing them out. 'Bout time. You couldn't put this one on for me too, could you?' The voice was American and somehow slightly familiar . . . .

Leo duly complied with the request and added the lady's chip to his own. A gasp from the table – another win! Again the vast pile of winnings approached but this time things went wrong. Leo and the lady simultaneously reached for their shares but, somehow mistiming this action in their excitement, they ended by knocking the whole lot on to the floor, where most rolled under the table. At once Leo went down on hands and knees to search. Reader, have you ever tried going *under* a roulette table? The main problem is that it is pitch dark. Thus, Leo was crawling about looking for chips like a manic Klondyke gold digger when, too late, he became aware that someone else was under there doing exactly the same. There was no time to take evasive action and with a tremendous crash both men collided, head to head. And so it was that, as they staggered up on their respective sides of the table, Leo addressed his first words to his former sovereign: 'You bloody blundering idiot! What the hell do you think you're doing?'

Well, it is distressing to think that the *tristesse* of the Duke of Windsor's exile should have included such a nightmare as being bawled at by Leo but at least His Royal Highness could reflect that his assailant had just won his wife a few bob. On the whole, though, I feel the incident merely underlines the obvious point that royal personages should never go travelling if at all possible. For them the truth is especially plain – travelling is synonymous not with tourism but with exile. The great 'progresses' of Elizabeth I are, of course, an important landmark – but one can hardly imagine the Virgin Queen going abroad. As for James I, he was terrified even to cross the border to assume his throne in England; his letters to his son Charles, in Madrid, to negotiate a possible Spanish

'. . . while giving the crate a massive kick . . .'

marriage are howls of despair by the non-traveller as he contemplates anyone going so far away, even for the gravest *raisons d'état*. No, the great lesson is that of Queen Victoria, wise in this as in so much else. Ruler of an empire on which the sun never sets, her furthest excursion from these shores was to the Isle of Wight. I mean, can you imagine the Empress of India actually *going* to India? Of course not – it might have led to a travelling disaster. Far better left to viceroys. The old Queen would readily have predicted the unfortunate experiences of Lady Curzon at the Great Durbar of 1903, at which she fell off the State Elephant, or rather got up one side only to slither down the other – as I did on my last attempt at riding an elephant many years ago . . . .

Perhaps even the ill-fated Czar Nicholas might have made it if he had really toughed it out instead of making constant plans to flee. The same might certainly be said of Charles I, and as for poor Louis and Marie Antoinette – look where the flight to Varennes got them! However, away with tragedy and back to mere embarrassment. The King of Norway was, of course, obliged to come to Britain to establish his government in exile for the duration of the last world war. Frankly, one feels that he had been through quite enough without the following incident to set the seal on the sadness of a king's travels. . . .

One day after the liberation in 1944, he was due to give an important speech to his countrymen from the BBC transmittors in London. He therefore arrived at Langham Place at the appointed hour and asked the commissionaire at the desk if he could be directed to Studio Thirteen. Do you know those commissionaires at the BBC by any chance? They are the most formidable body of public servants in the world – they always remind me of the door-keeper Osmin in the *Seraglio* – a sort of surly savagery which one feels cannot be natural has somehow been inculcated (by whom? Lord Reith?). Anyway, the King received the same response as the rest of us. A narrowing of the eyes, a pursing of the lips. 'And what's the name, sir, if you please?' 'Well, as a matter of fact

I'm the King of Norway.' 'I see. Well, if you'll take a seat here, sir, I'll just go and make enquiries.' 'Yes, but please excuse me, the programme is nearly due. I really must go to the studio at once.' 'Well now, all in good time, sir. You just take it easy for a while and I won't be long.' Dismayed, the King sits down to wait. Several minutes pass before Osmin returns with an expression in which suspicion battles with incredulity to deliver the immortal line: 'I beg your pardon, sir, but which country did you say you were king of?'

Certain it is, then, that kings should not travel – but does this necessarily imply that we lesser mortals should not do so either? I put the question to my ultra-monarchist friend, Leo Gardiner. His reply was typical. 'It is not for the subject to attempt to *learn* from the actions of his sovereign. All he owes him is *blind obedience.* . . .'

Inanimate Travellers
and Immovable Beasts

If royal disasters reign then what about the string of disasters associated with travel by inanimate – or at least non-human – objects?

The wrath of grapes

Wine, as is well known, does not travel. Attempts to make it do so have invariably resulted in the production of such bizarre disasters as sherry – the ruin of Mother, the British Empire, and no doubt many another worthy cause.

'Wine maketh glad the heart of man.' This admirable sentiment merely proclaims wine to be a pleasant adjunct to civilized living; a far cry indeed from the endless snobbish waffle promulgated by the new breed of wine/travel writers, let alone the sort of wine nonsense perfectly exemplified by the ludicrous annual *Nouveau* Beaujolais race. (One wonders if the participants are aware that this thin, vinegarish liquid was merely what the vineyard owners gave the labourers, doubtless in order to keep them sufficiently befuddled not to notice the size of their wage packets.) How very different from a Beaujolais of a decent, not too recent year, actually drunk on the spot. The truth is that today most wine has done so much travelling that hardly anyone can remember what it really tastes like any more. The EEC regulations even encourage such amazing anomalies as the bulk purchase of wine at auctions in London, followed by its re-export back to France, where an ingenious wine merchant can sell it at a price lower than that of the same wine had it never left the country.

Given this, it must be a painful trial to be a true wine connoisseur today. Dreadful vintages abound in the most unexpected places. For instance, a high point of my last visit to Italy was an invitation from one of the younger knights of Malta for drinks at the Order's castle at Mugione, on Lake Trasimene, north of Rome. It was particularly exciting to be offered a glass of the Knight's own Mugione wine since for many centuries it has been their privilege to supply this wine to the Vatican for liturgical use in the Papal Mass. Naturally I was all agog to taste a vintage with connotations of such sacred and historical interest. Imagine then my horror as I struggled with the most utterly undrinkable wine I have ever tried – and I have battled with some pretty horrible red ink in various parts of Italy. I tried to look suitably appreciative but my host collapsed with laughter. 'So you think it's horrible too? You should have seen Prince Guy de Polignac's face when we made him try it. Fortunately few Popes are interested in wine, with the exception of Pius XII. He used to accept our weekly bottle with a noble resignation. "Ah well," he would sigh, "they say Mass wine never hurt a priest . . . ."'

One who suffered a wine travelling disaster on a major scale is a certain well-known Australian racehorse owner and trainer. Based in the Lambourne Valley, he also maintains a substantial establishment on the West Coast of Australia and maintains many contacts with France. A noted wine enthusiast, he has built up a superb cellar, kept primarily at Lambourne. Only recently did he decide to bring a selection of the finest bottles out to Australia; he recently married an Australian lady and decided to spend more time 'down under'.

He was, of course, well aware of the dangers of wine travel disasters and set about overcoming the problem in his own way. Naturally, he disliked the notion of commercial airlines; he would hire his own aircraft and, yet further, commission the design and construction of a special crate, precisely regulated in terms of temperature and humidity and with a completely original electronic giroscopic balancing mechanism which would keep the bottles safe from even the slightest vibration.

In all these arrangements we see once again the usual hubris which leads to travel disaster. The route selected was via New Guinea, notorious for unpredictable climatic conditions. This time they ran into something even worse than the usual cyclones; this is the rare weather phenomenon known to seamen as a 'line squall', in which dead calm is suddenly followed by a force eight gale with sea-level cloud cover. Somehow the giroscopic wine stabilizer survived even this test. They landed in Hong Kong with the plane shaken virtually into its component pieces but the wine apparently perfectly all right – that is, until it was transshipped to a commercial flight for the final leg to Australia. At this point human folly and ineptitude succeeded where the elements had failed.

The new captain was Australian; he was truculent, he was furious at the unnecessary delay to his flight, he was not a little drunk. He demanded to see the secret extra cargo, the loading of which had kept him waiting for three hours. It consisted, apparently, simply of a huge crate ... but what was that? It was emitting a curious, vaguely electrical purring sound. Frightful visions of bombs and hi-jackers flashed through his mind. With meticulous care he bent to the task of removing the board furthest away from the diabolical humming. It took him half an hour's cautious work with his penknife but at last it came clear, to reveal serried racks of musty-looking old bottles. The anti-climax was too much. Furiously seizing the first bottle he could see – a priceless Château Latour – he smashed the top and consumed the contents, while giving the crate a massive kick. This, of course, upset the giroscope, and the flight finally touched down in Perth with its exquisite cargo either broken or undrinkable.

'Tortoises produce serum . . . . Innoculation of the whole German people . . .'

Treasures in transit

To travel is to change one's nature. If, in the case of wine, we agree that this can only be for the worse, what of works of art? Surely the same applies. How utterly different is the trecento diptych in its place in the Italian church for which it was painted or the Vandyck portrait in a great seventeenth-century house, instead of on the odiously immaculate walls of a modern museum. Most museums are, in any case, like the Louvre, in large measure repositories of stolen goods or at best objects bought from others by the use of inadmissible pressure – the Elgin Marbles, for instance, or the magnificent early Italian paintings bought in Victorian times by English collectors who went round the villages calling, 'Bring out your Madonnas'. Even where that is not so, most of the pictures seem to be screaming, 'I don't belong here. Take me away.' Not that I think this should be applied too literally – the court had scant sympathy for James Robinson, the greatest Oxford kleptomaniac of my generation, when arrested at London airport boarding a flight to France with an important Watteau from an English country house wrapped round his waist. He claimed that he was simply 'repatriating' it.

Clearly, however, there will have to be far tighter controls even on the legal movement of works of art if the entire remaining Western patrimony is not to end up in Malibu or – worse – stored permanently in vaults, like cases of wine, to be used as mere financial collateral in the auction game. (I have myself heard, in Paris, someone enquiring of their favourite gallery owner, as of a stockbroker, 'What are Bonnard's points today? He's standing at seventy-three! Buy! Dufy? Slipped to sixty-eight? Sell! ', referring to pictures he had never seen and had no intention of seeing.

It is, however, delightful to contemplate a proper disaster connected with the attempted export of a picture. This took place in the early 1950s, when both Italian and American customs were making every possible effort to prevent the outflow of major Italian paintings to the USA. The normal technique was to cover your beautiful Duccio, or whatever, with a futuristic modern painting which, on arrival, could be scraped off. On this occasion, so the charming story runs, our American collector got his masterpiece to the States in this way and sent it to his restorer for removal of the top layer. Nothing happened for ages. Puzzled, he sent the restorer a telegram: HOW ARE YOU GETTING ON? The reply came immediately: HAVE SCRAPED OFF FUTURIST DAUB REMOVED FAKE DUCCIO AM DOWN TO PORTRAIT OF MUSSOLINI STOP WHERE DO I STOP?

Animals – their beastly bad luck

Thus our indictment of travel builds up. Wine sits undrunk in Bond Street cellars; pictures languish, wrenched out of context in remote museums or Parisian vaults; and what of animals? They sit around, wretched captives, in that most grotesque of museums, the zoo. Here at least we have used our vast ingenuity in the field of travel to some effect. Like medieval armies, we have taken substantial prisoners and brought them home in chains; we salve our bad conscience only with such modest works of art as 'Tarzan' and 'King Kong'. We are even prepared to enjoy a degenerate frisson at the thought of two enormous animals, pandas or giant bears for example, mating in these appalling conditions – animals for whom the norm is to trudge across 1000 miles of frozen tundra in search of the right partner (and then, be it noted, to remain with them in permanent fidelity). No wonder some of the greatest hoaxes and absurd 'scares' concern zoos – in the mid-fifties, for instance, a young reporter's joke headline: 'Leopard loose in Central Park' caused yet another panic evacuation of the city, while in wartime . . . .

London 1943. All the zoo animals were thoroughly secured against the bombing (for our peace of mind rather than

71

theirs). The same was, naturally, true of zoos in Central Europe. Animals wouldn't, after all, be going anywhere in wartime. Utter panic, therefore, in the Ministry of Economic Warfare Intelligence Unit when it became known that a train had just left Vienna for Berlin (this at the height of Hitler's Russian offensive) with a cargo of tortoises. The information was re-checked; brave men risked their lives to make certain of it. There was no doubt – the train contained a very large number of tortoises. Nothing else.

As so often in wartime, this unintelligible piece of information provoked first incredulity, then slight worry, then absolute panic. For what possible reason could the Reich, at this crucial juncture, be devoting resources vital for the transport of men and munitions to this humble objective? Of what use would tortoises be to those who had invented the *Blitzkrieg?* The Ministry's Evaluation Committee sat far into the night, joined, as in all cases of dire emergency, by an ever-growing number of officials. Bomber Command, the Chiefs of Staff, a direct line to the Prime Minister, a bevy of scientific advisers. It was one of these who, at about two in the morning, produced the answer. 'Tortoises . . . produce serum for certain drugs . . . . Inoculation . . . inoculation of the whole German people . . . germ warfare! ' Imagine the scene – what a night! It was not until six the following morning that someone for whom tiredness had replaced hysteria had the wit to say, 'Yes, but do we actually *know* this? Before we disturb Mr Churchill, I suggest that we wait at least until the tortoises have arrived in Berlin.' And so it was. Twenty-four hours later, reliable sources revealed that the tortoises' journey had been scheduled by the zoo officials involved four years before, in 1939, before the war broke out. Subsequent events had not cancelled the arrangement. The tortoises were just doing their own thing – travelling at that moment, in contrast to the Führer's divisions or British Intelligence, definitely faster than the hare.

In fact, animals are themselves conspicuously superior to human beings when it comes to travelling. Migrating birds

'Renaissance, with slight mannerist tendencies . . .'

and fish find their direction with an ease which makes our efforts look pathetic. Furthermore, shutting them up in zoos seems a poor way to reward them for having made all our own travels not only possible but enjoyable, since they are the ideal travelling companions, never losing their passports or travellers' cheques, or spoiling one's appreciation of a fine fifteenth-century façade with some inept comment.

Stephenson's delightful donkey, for instance, comes from a distinguished line stretching back to the ass on which Christ chose to enter Jerusalem; indeed the humble, useful creature provides a link with the Mahometan world, for did not the Prophet ascend to heaven on his sacred, winged ass, Balaam? The Islamic world, incidentally, is surely far more realistic about travelling than the Christian, but then you would be, wouldn't you, if your basic means of transportation was the camel rather than the horse. Camels, like zebras, never get broken in; Kipling captures their anti-travel spirit perfectly in his: 'Can't, don't, shan't, won't/Pass it along the line./Somebody's pack has slid from his back/wish it were only mine'. Many explanations have been offered for the infinitely superior and condescending look on the camel's face; legend has it that this is due to the fact that Allah has revealed to man, in the Koran, 999 of his 1000 names but the thousandth only to the camel. But I think it's just as likely that the creature is merely thinking, pityingly, of the ludicrously pointless journeys on which it is constantly expected to embark.

Dog's tales . . . .

Although a faithful dog is a good creature and a friend of man, he is essentially a stay-at-home; for him travelling is invariably a disaster. Nothing, for example, is more distressing than to witness the fate of any foreign breed, particularly one of the larger varieties, when brought from England or Germany to Italy or Spain. The poor creature is now in a world completely devoid of dogginess and dog tradition. *You* try, for instance, telling an Italian that in England people habitually give their dogs meat (and, indeed, two of my best friends obtained a fine weekly roast by asking at Harrod's Food Hall if there were by any chance any scraps left over for their desperately sick wolfhound. 'You see, on Social Security it is not that we might not eat, it is that we cannot face the look in poor dumb Timothy's eyes.')

In Italy, however, Timothy would be lucky to get a bowl of spaghetti a day, a fact which accounts for the vast number of borzois and Dobermann pinschers with most of their hair fallen out, trotting listlessly along the streets of Rome and Milan behind their bejewelled mistresses.

Usually, of course, the poor beasts eventually lie down and die, though there was a most distressing case when I was last in Rome involving a film producer who felt that a pet leopard might make his Parioli flat that much more chic. Eventually he managed to buy one from the Rome Opera, in which it had done yeoman service in various productions of *Aida*, though naturally drugged into a state of goofy harmlessness. Having obtained this prize, the producer put it out on the terrace outside his drawing room where it would prowl majestically up and down outside the plate glass windows to many an 'Oooh' and 'Ah' from his lady guests. After a few days, during which it was given nothing but spaghetti, the producer went off for a location shoot over the weekend, forgetting about the poor creature entirely. Alas, it was not he who was first back to the flat on the Monday morning – it was his cleaning lady, to whom he had, of course, forgotten to mention the beast's existence . . . . She went straight to the balcony door and flung it open. He got back to Rome that afternoon to find his pet fast asleep on the drawing room floor surrounded by a pile of bones, replete at last after a good square meal.

Returning to dogs for a moment, I did once see the denouement of a crisis in which a dog underwent an experience one thinks of as essentially reserved for human beings – kidnapping. On a misty November evening in

Venice, in a humble fisherman's bar off the Campo Goldoni, I came across an unlikely figure. It was James Fawcett, an immensely wealthy young Texan whom I had met at a party a week or so before. But the ebullient James of the party had quite disappeared; in his place there was this haggard shadow of a man pouring himself with trembling hand glass after glass of neat Grappa from a litre bottle. 'My dear James, what is the matter?' 'It's my dawg,' he muttered, staring into his glass. 'My dawg, they've taken my dawg!' 'What dog? I didn't know you had a dog. You mean you brought a dog with you all the way from the United States?' 'Listen, he's called Poppet, he's a bassett hound. He goes everywhere with me. He . . . . ' Sobs choked him and it was some time before I could extract the complete story.

It transpired that on the evening in question, James had taken Poppet with him on a quick trip to the corner bar for some cigarettes. A bassett hound is very rare in Italy and Poppet was well known – indeed he was the talk of the entire district. James decided to have a beer and fell into conversation with the barman. He had noticed that when he entered the bar it contained three or four 'sinister-looking types' – as he put it. (I ask you, who on earth doesn't look sinister on a murky November evening in Venice? He might have meant anybody from the Cardinal to Peggy Guggenheim.) Anyway, when he turned round the bar was empty. No sinister types and no Poppet. The barman of course, being a Venetian barman, noticed nothing, just like the concierge at the Luna Hotel when, in Venice's last great murder, the Countess Tarnowska put six revolver shots into her lover in the next-door bedroom and then fled dishevelled past his desk in the hallway with the smoking gun in her hand.

The police had been sympathetic but not very hopeful. Could Poppet swim, they wondered? So easy to miss one's footing in the dark. Or perhaps Poppet had spotted a cat and given chase. Far more likely, James opined, that Poppet, on confronting an average Venetian cat, would have fled in abject terror. Anyway, an all-points alarm for Poppet had so far yielded no results and I must confess that James's dramatic kidnap theory struck me even then as just possible.

The next day the *Gazzettino di Venezia*, that most delightful of local newspapers, published a moving plea by James to anyone who knew Poppet's whereabouts. James would ensure that anyone returning the dog would 'have no cause to regret his action'. (Italian law is rather strict about the offer of a specific reward where it might appear to condone a crime.) There were photographs of both James and Poppet on the front page of the paper – this in the world of the *Gazzettino* was a major news story – plus a lengthy leading article deploring this new example of the sickening crime wave 'holding the city', I quote, 'in a grip of terror'.

I went round to see James that evening to proffer some whisky and consolation and to see if the newspaper publicity had produced any results. Consequently I was there with him when shortly before midnight his telephone rang. My presence was fortunate since James's Italian was sketchy and his interlocutor spoke no English. I was called in to interpret. Greatly to my surprise, the voice at the other end evidently did not belong to some scarfaced mafioso threatening to send James one of Poppet's long floppy ears if his demands were not met. Instead, an educated, cultured voice informed me that I was speaking to Dr X, one of the best-known dentists in Venice. It was he who had found Poppet wandering around in the mist, evidently lost. He had taken him home and looked after him. (Ghastly visions of the pampered Poppet trying to force down the remains of the good doctor's *fettuccine* flashed through my mind.) However, I thanked him profusely on James's behalf and suggested that perhaps we might come round and collect Poppet there and then. 'Of course,' agreed the doctor, providing that James would be kind enough to pay the bill first. I courteously enquired how much would be appropriate for board and accommodation for one dog for ten days or so. The reply was so outrageous that at first I thought I must have misunderstood the number of noughts he had in mind – it would have been about right if the doctor had managed to kidnap James himself. Knowing how important it is in Italian negotiations to stall at the right moment, I requested the doctor to drop us a bill in writing and politely rang off before James had a chance to deliver some Texan fire and brimstone down the telephone.

Next morning James rang me. The doctor had dropped the bill in during the night. It was almost entirely for professional services rendered and explained in technical but intelligible language that the doctor had felt so distressed by the state of Poppet's teeth that he had made the following adjustments – fillings, extractions, cleaning, polishing, etc., etc. Unfortunately, there could be no question of Poppet's return until these fees were paid.

It took some time to get James under control. 'I'm gonna bust in there and get his cat. I'm gonna send it back to him paw by paw. I'm gonna make a recording of its teeth being torn out. He plays rough – I play rough.' This was actually the reaction required. I put through a quick call to the American Consulate and explained that James was now completely over the top. They understood; they promised to intervene at an official level.

We did not have to wait long. It was barely twenty minutes later when an amazing noise caused us to rush to the balcony. An enormous high-speed police patrol boat containing at least eight heavily armed *carabinieri* zoomed past James's window down the Grand Canal and turned off into the little Rio where the doctor lived, in a sheet of spray. Ten minutes later it reappeared and came charging down the Canal towards us, but by this time four of them were sitting in a row with the weird elongated form of Poppet lying across their laps. They stopped at the Fondamenta and handed him over in as operatic a scene as I have ever witnessed in Italy. There was saluting, back-slapping, laughter, tears. I expected someone to start singing at any moment. I need hardly say that the morning ended with a desperate search round the Venetian butchers' shops for a couple of pounds of steak worthy of Poppet's palate after his terrible deprivations.

Needless to say we couldn't find any and ended by having to get some from Harry's Bar.

From Immovable Beast to Movable Feast

How interesting it is that France has produced so few 'travellers'. Could you translate into French the words: 'Dr Livingstone, I presume?' Obviously not. The French don't go travelling on this crazy basis. Even at the height of the last century, French possessions abroad were seen not so much as part of an empire but as evidence of France's *'Mission Civilisatrice'*.

Thus France has no Colombus, no Marco Polo, no Drake, no Scott. Instead, it has Papillon, whose stupendous life story consists simply of an attempt to get out of a French penal colony as soon as possible. Even the great Napoleon was defeated in Spain and Russia; the entire expedition to Egypt reveals a general not a traveller. It is quite simple – in the nineteenth century, England was the sort of place you left as fast as you could; France you stayed in, if possible, all your life.

This, of course, remains true. The world may change; empires may come and go (and I notice I had not even heard of a third of the countries competing in the 1984 Olympic Games) but certain things remain immovable. In the Restaurant des Ministères in the Rue du Bac in Paris you can still have lobster *flambé* in 1914 Armagnac, and the Sainte Chapelle still looks as magnificent as ever. Since there is no point in leaving France – Victor Hugo insisted: 'Everything that exists elsewhere exists in Paris' – it follows that the French are hopeless travellers who would far rather congregate in a Club Méditerranée than attempt the act of international tourism with its attendant risks.

Scanty knowledge of Dante

Let me illustrate. I was sitting one day in the Piazza Santa Croce in Florence with the distinguished art historian, Charles Hope, one of the organizers of the 1984 Venice Exhibition in London. It was early in the morning and we were consuming a Florentine working man's breakfast of chicken livers on hot toast washed down by the odd glass of Chianti, while contemplating the enormous nineteenth-century statue of Dante which dominates the square. This grotesque sculpture must actually be the only truly ugly object in Florence, positioned immediately outside the sacred basilica with its sublime Giottos. It's almost as grotesque as Sir Basil Spence's British Embassy in Rome immediately adjoining Michelangelo's Porta Pia.

However, our analysis of this repulsive object was suddenly interrupted. An enormous Peugeot estate car suddenly entered the square and drew to a halt beside us. Its number plates proclaimed Paris but its passengers, evidently a family, suggested one of those chic suburbs which surround the capital: Neuilly, perhaps. The father leapt from the car with the look that only the French manage to achieve when travelling – exhausted, triumphant, but, above all, supremely patronizing. Pointing to the statue with a heroic gesture probably modelled on David's painting of Napoleon at the Bridge of Lodi, he exclaimed to his little flock, 'C'est Michelange, ça!' Alas his effect was only marred by the presence of these two typically rude and ignorant Englishmen who, for some unknown reason, were falling about laughing.

It's only the President . . . .

It is indeed ironic that French should have emerged as the traditional language of diplomacy. One of the consequences of this fact is that you expect French diplomats to be more effective than others – better travelled, more sophisticated, less likely to get into a mess. But if that is what you think, you definitely ought to meet my friend Maurice. Without a doubt France has no more charming representative, but I trust none so terribly unfortunate in his travels.

Take the very first night on his first posting abroad, to Tokyo. He was asked to be on call for the Embassy telephone in the unlikely event of some immense crisis developing during the night – a tiresome chore which the Under-Secretaries have to take in rotation. Just Maurice's luck – he was fast asleep when the phone rang at four in the morning. He was still getting over the effects of jet lag (travel again, you see) and was therefore even more exhausted than is normal at 4 a.m. He grabbed the telephone with a sleepy hand and launched into a tirade of verbal abuse at the 'dirty *cochon*' who could have the nerve to wake him at this unearthly hour. 'Who the hell are you anyway?' he demanded when the stream of epithets ran out. A voice cold as ice on the other end of the line simply replied, '*Ici parle Charles de Gaulle*' . . . .

'Next time, go for the mother . . . . '

Well, no doubt a soldier president could forgive a bit of barrack-room bluntness in place of diplomatic suavity. Maurice's next gaffe, however, was on a very different level. He had been transferred to London where he found among other things that his recent divorce had made him a highly eligible bachelor all over again. Unfortunately, however, although Maurice's English is excellent, it took him some time to master some of the more subtle implications of an English social situation. The following for instance baffled him.

He was having pre-dinner drinks with the director of one of our greatest museums, his charming wife and their radiantly beautiful daughter, by whom Maurice was instantaneously bewitched. He was therefore both puzzled and deeply disappointed when as the dinner hour arrived the girl said goodnight to all present and disappeared upstairs. 'She's got such a lot of homework to do, you see,' said her mother. Maurice: 'You mean she's studying for some exam?' 'Oh yes, but she does work tremendously hard. Her French teacher is especially pleased with her.' Maurice: 'But I should be delighted to give her some conversation practice myself.' 'How terribly kind of you but I'm sure you'd be much too busy,' murmurs the mother, looking distinctly puzzled.

Even by now Maurice still hadn't got it. The object of his passion was simply one of those girls who look much more grown up than they are. She wasn't an eighteen-year-old student but a thirteen-year-old schoolgirl. Hence his next moves began to cause the mother not just puzzlement but real alarm. He tried inviting all three to dinner *chez lui* (he was, of course, baffled when the mother said it was too late for Veronica to be up). He took the mother out to lunch alone, was invited back to dinner again by the family, reinvited them all to a drinks party at which he managed to talk to Veronica alone in a corner for half an hour.

Finally, one Saturday afternoon, he made his move. He rang up and got the mother on the line. 'Could I speak to Veronica, please?' The mother sounded completely astonished but finally went off to fetch her. 'Veronica, *ma trés chère*,' purrs Maurice down the line, 'I wondered if you could spare an evening for a little dinner with me at the Gavroche some time next week? Then we might go on to a nightclub or something – or maybe a little gambling. Are you fond of roulette? A beautiful girl like you is bound to bring me luck.' 'Well it's very kind of you, Monsieur, but of course I'll have to ask Mummy.' 'My dear, how terribly polite of you but surely hardly necessary. I *am* a friend of your family after all. Anyway ring me back this evening and tell me which day.'

It was well before the evening, in fact less than half an hour later, that Maurice's phone rang and all hell broke loose. It was the ambassador's wife on the line. 'Maurice, I can hardly bring myself to speak to you, you disgusting, repellent pervert. I didn't realize your tastes extended to thirteen-year-old schoolgirls. At least you might have the grace to keep your repulsive desires to yourself. You, an accredited diplomatic representative of France *en poste* in a foreign country, you make advances to a child who is the daughter of one of its most distinguished cultural figures .... Words fail me. I've had to use all my influence to prevent your immediate recall to Paris.' 'But, Madame, I did not realize ....' 'Did not realize! Well, let me give you a word of advice. Next time you're in doubt, *go for the mother, you blockhead.*' Thus were Maurice's gallantries sorted into a less lethal course and further diplomatic disasters averted.

Carnivals and Crusades

From poseurs and perverts to parties and pilgrimages . . . .

Fiesta or fiasco?

We have touched upon the horrors attendant on travels in Latin America, but surely there must be a more cheerful side? What of the carnival, for instance? Isn't that a splendid explosion of Latin *joie de vivre*, in contrast to the dreariness of the Anglo-Saxon? Surely this is an ecstasy in which even he can join – can, if only for a little, abandon his tiresome sense of responsibility?

Alas, nothing could be further from the truth than this absurd approach. To attend a carnival is to invite travel disaster of unsurpassable magnitude. You must remember first that during the carnival period in most Central and South American countries all business transactions, including banking, stop for weeks rather than days. What price now for a full wallet of travellers' cheques, cleverly made out in Swiss francs? Uncashable even if you retain them (and you are ninety-five per cent certain to lose them anyway), they won't get you anywhere when the manager of the local American Express office is himself cavorting around town for three consecutive weeks, completely drunk, dressed as an iguana . . . .

You must remember, further, that carnival is exceptionally dangerous. A Rio carnival with only 400 deaths, for instance, is generally reckoned a pretty tame affair.

Gala garb

Even if you decide to attend, you might make a mistake – and that's remarkably easy to do. The eternal question, 'What on earth am I going to wear?', for instance, here takes on an alarming new meaning. My friend, the painter and designer James Reeve, staying in Port au Prince, was unaware that at the great Haitian carnival you do not don your costume until the second day. The first is entirely formal. He thus turned up for the pre-carnival part chez one of the great Haitian hostesses imagining that it was all going to be like *The Violins of St Jacques*. (See the disastrous effect of reading too many travel books!) James arrived dressed as Death, in a terrifying costume made for him in New York (one of whose main features was a number of artificial dead flies), to find the party immaculate in white tie and tails. It was with great difficulty that he explained to his astonished host that this miscalculation was in no sense intended as a calculated and insulting allusion to his country's policies . . . .

Another carnival visitor whose dress sense momentarily failed was no less a traveller than Freya Stark. How often has that intrepid lady taken us in imagination to some of the roughest and remotest parts of the world; but it was in the civilized atmosphere of the Venetian carnival that this mishap took place – and exquisite illustration of the fact that the real horror of travelling lies so often in intense embarrassment rather than direct danger.

The year was 1959; the carnival party there given in the vast Palazzo Labia by the Conte de Bestigui. Everyone who was there, let alone all (such as myself) who merely wish they had been, agree that this must have been the bash of the century, or at least since the 1910 party at which the legendary Boni de Castellane hung every single tree in the Bois de Boulogne with coloured lights. Fancy dress optional. Immediately all the greatest couturiers from Rome to New York – Erté, Christian Bérard, Pucinelli – sat down to produce some of

'... "I bet it's there!" And it was ...'

their most lavish creations. Freya Stark, however, British to the last, decided to make her own costume. Correctly calculating that the other guests would opt for the eighteenth century or thereabouts, she decided to come as a medieval knight, in cardboard armour painted grey.

Thus attired, she drove to Venice from her home in Asolo twenty miles away. Her first move was to find a rather worried gondolier to take her up the Grand Canal to the Labia – and here disaster struck. The Canal is choppy in February and boarding a craft at night as unstable as a gondola is not particularly easy at the best of times, let alone in full armour. In she fell; the gondolier fished her out, but the short journey proved absolutely fatal to her costume. By the time she arrived the grey paint was pouring down her breastplate, clearly revealing the legend 'Cinzano' underneath. It also ran into the area below her helmet, causing it to stick immovably to her shoulders.

Unfortunately, the party was in full swing when she arrived; the other guests, disporting themselves under that most superb of Tiepolo ceilings, stopped in amazement at the appearance of this astonishing, dripping apparition. The Conte de Bestigui, however – always the perfect host – stepped forward. 'Madame,' he said, 'I see that, like a true knight, you have stormed my castle through the moat. But do not worry – I have several alternative costumes in my wardrobe. Perhaps you would care to come as a negro pageboy?'

After enjoying the vision of Miss Stark thus suddenly translated from knight to blackamoor, the guests could now turn their attention to the party's next excitement – the arrival of Ava Gardner naked on a camel . . . .

A shanghai to be ashamed of . . . .

Another aspect of carnival where the untutored visitor may well fall into error is that of the traditional practical jokes

'. . . he was going to find the mummified body of Egypt's most sacred
king . . .'

which are linked to the ancient concept of the Mask. The only rule is to laugh your head off at all the absurd practical jokes played on you while being extremely careful about reciprocating. For instance, let us leave the Great Carnival of Venice for that at Burano, a tiny island in the Venetian lagoon whose inhabitants are entirely devoted to fishing, lace-making and drinking (not necessarily in that order). The contrast with the Venetian carnival is delightful. The Venice carnival, like Rio, has become essentially a spectacle, the revels of which are deeply related to TV camera angles; Burano remains exactly the explosion of joy one looks for, and is still hardly known to the tourist (please don't all rush there). On Burano your worry is not the state of your cardboard armour – here you may well get pushed in, 'just for fun'. However, it is important not to misread the mood, as you shall hear.

Carnival 1974. I decided, with a friend in Venice, to get up a small party of four to try the Burano carnival. We would go there in style – by water taxi – and in the most correct traditional manner also *en travesti* and masked, our girl-friends magnificent Marlene Dietrichs in top hat and tails and we two men looking, if I may quote the ladies' catty comments, like a couple of blowsy old whores they had picked up in some grotty sailors' bar down the Riva. We were also armed – at the whim of my friend – with extremely realistic-looking, and sounding, toy pistols.

Eventually the water taxi arrived and we all set off – a merry party from Harry's Bar, where our appearance had already created a *succès de scandale*. The journey is less than half an hour in a fast motorboat but the Venetian lagoon is a strange place, especially at night; the lights of the city recede, the wind gets up, you suddenly remember that you are not on a lake but on an only partially landlocked part of the Adriatic Sea. Our motorboat very wisely started slowing down, whereupon my friend, Alan, struck. Leaping forward to the driver's seat, he produced his pistol and announced that we were, in fact, terrorists planning to hi-jack his boat. Alas, what a terrible joke at that particular moment – the first great

Italian kidnappings, the emergence of the Red Brigades, the tragic death of Aldo Moro. The driver took it completely seriously, was absolutely terrified. The boat lurched out of control as he raised his hands. 'Where would you like me to go?' he stammered. 'Have you enough petrol for Yugoslavia?' 'Well, *signor*, we could always try . . . .' Indeed, he had half-turned the boat towards the open sea when gales of laughter from the back reminded him that this was carnival, and we were merely naïve travellers trying unsuccessfully to grasp its spirit.

'Would the real Fidel Castro please stand up . . . ?'

That you must, however, be large-hearted when the joke is played against you is excellently demonstrated by an adventure of my late friend, Caroline McCullough. As a young journalist she went to Cuba, heavily laden with the primitive sound equipment the BBC were then using, to try for an interview with Fidel. She arrived in the middle of carnival time, or at least some wild Castroite popular festival equivalent to it, to find the entire airport awash with cheering crowds. These were, however, there to meet not Caroline but the new French ambassador, arriving on the next plane. (Indeed, his reaction on first hearing the Marseillaise in a cha-cha-cha rhythm might well stand as our motto: *'Mais c'est trop surréaliste pour être vrai'.*)

Naturally she was delighted when the impressive-looking truck arrived to whisk her to a country villa for the Castro meeting, and enthralled when, after a suitable interval, the bearded, battle-fatigued leader appeared. The interview was an absolute triumph – in fact it went on until the tape ran out, though selected passages had, as expected, to be excised before presentation to the BBC in London ('Ah, Caroline, our Cuban girls are beautiful, yes, but you with your blonde hair, your bright blue eyes, ah, ah' – 'No please, not *now*, Comrade

President, I mean, please, couldn't we continue about land reform?' etc.). And yet there was something else in Castro's manner, something which made Caroline feel increasingly that she was being teased. It emerged right at the end, when she finally gave in and accepted her interlocutor's invitation to dinner. 'And now, since you've been such a good girl, I shall also extend you an invitation to meet my brother, the President . . . . ' Poor Caroline had given an entire interview to Raoul in the belief that he was Fidel.

Hardly a disaster perhaps; Caroline did eventually get her interview with Fidel and Raoul was, of course, also himself quite interesting. Rather, a joke in the carnival spirit, one of whose main motifs is mistaken identity.

'Give us back our shrines – or at least let us visit them'

Let us now consider another very important and ancient form of celebration and travel, again dogged by disaster. This is the world of pilgrimage. We have already mentioned *The Canterbury Tales*; it is of interest that Chaucer does not describe the arrival of the pilgrims or their reaction to St Thomas's shrine. In fact, for many centuries pilgrims were shown part of the sword belonging to one of the knights who dispatched that 'turbulent priest', but the story has been subtly censored in order to elevate it from the realm of squalid political murder. The impression given, at least to the foreign pilgrims who leave us an account, is that the archbishop, far from being done to death at the foot of his own altar, was formally beheaded, presumably after a suitably corrupt trial.

This simplified and naïve notion of the light shed by the story on the relations between church and state is typical of the way pilgrimage centres treat whatever is the actual object of the pilgrimage. Commercial rivalry is the main consideration – why should a pilgrim visit you if you've only got one of the thorns from the Crown of Thorns, while Piacenza has eight and Monza ten? If what you have is, as at Canterbury, the memory of a recent event, it must be simplified; if a relic, it must be more efficacious than its nearest rival; if an apparition – of the Virgin or of a saint – more recent. This gives you a chance of luring away the local pilgrim trade in your direction and, believe me, not the most cut-throat competition in modern bucket-shop air fares can begin to rival that between medieval pilgrim shrines.

Down in Calabria, the little town of Messinella had for ages been the proud possessor of a phial containing one of Christ's tears, when the nearby village of Pinolo suddenly came up in the thirteenth century with the exciting rediscovery of the fact that its church ran to something just as sacred but even less tangible – one of St Joseph's sighs. Controversy about the authenticity of these rival attractions reached a high point when the Bishop of Messinella proclaimed from the pulpit that to encapsulate one of St Joseph's sighs in a phial was theologically impossible. The inhabitants of Pinolo responded with an armed attack on the town; the bishop was, after all, striking not merely at their precious relic but at all the ancillary spin-off industries deriving from it, notably the countless pilgrims' inns and rest houses in the vicinity.

Curiously, they need not have worried unduly, for one of the most intriguing facts about shrines and relics is that the veneration they excite is barely connected with their authenticity – indeed, constant denunciations, preferably Papal, may well be a positive advantage. Thousands continue to flock to see 'Padre Pio', though it is now by no means certain whether he is alive or dead; in any case, that part of southern Italy is full of hundreds of false Padre Pios, complete with beard and stigmata, who will be delighted to confess you for a suitable fee, after which you could always drop into the local church to see the wood for the three tabernacles which St Peter proposed to make, and even – needless to say in Pinolo – the cornerstone which the builders rejected . . . .

In loos . . .

One thing, however, is to be noted about travelling in these parts. It is imperative always to make use of any adequate toilet facilities you happen to come across, for who knows when you will find another. I personally use the system developed by Norman Douglas on the travels which resulted in *Old Calabria* and *South Wind*. He would send in his companion to investigate anything they came across in the way of a loo and report back in art-historical terms. 'Renaissance with slight Mannerist tendencies', 'glorified early Baroque', but more usually 'very early medieval', 'provincial Romanesque'. The worst was in some very humble Calabrian village where Douglas's friend Orioli came running back in seconds, 'My God, this one's *Etrusco!*'

. . . and in lieu of

By the way, though Douglas was undoubtedly quite the most inspired and erudite travel writer who ever lived, I wouldn't take all his recommendations too literally today. It is, for instance, true that the ideal accompaniment for wild boar is (incredibly) chocolate sauce, and also that the best *boisson* for this dish (authentically Roman, one of the few) is dry white wine. Ask for all this in, say, Otello's in the Via della Croce in Rome and you will be hailed as a connoisseur. But just try, as I did, to go to Douglas's lengths and demand that they produce scales and weigh any wine you leave, and refund you the difference. 'What do I do, *Signore*?' enquired the waiter witheringly. 'Deduct the result from the bill on your American Express card?' And yet sixty years ago this immemorial practice was still common. Ah well, '*autres temps, autres moeurs.*'

'It is nice to know that one has something in common with Goethe.'

Package to Purgatory

Returning to pilgrim shrines for a moment. It does seem sad that Reformation, Reason and the nineteenth century have left the British Isles so depleted of this sort of thing, but there is a noble and moving exception in Lough Derg, in Ireland, still the scene of one of Europe's last surviving penitential pilgrimages. Repeated abolitions by numerous Popes has only added to its lustre, though today the various penances last only for three days; nonetheless Lough Derg is the ultimate in travel disasters you voluntarily seek out for yourself – as if travel wasn't sufficiently penitential anyway. Today you have yourself rowed out to Holy Island, where you spend three gruelling days and nights, one of them in the extremely alarming cave in which the Irish knight Owen experienced a terrifying vision of Purgatory in 1153. You are allowed nothing to eat or drink and spend one of the days up to your waist in water . . . . I know all this from a friend, a London solicitor of otherwise perfectly normal habits, who does this every year. Knowing only that he went regularly to the same Irish lough, but unaware of the circumstances, I asked him – in a classic travel gaffe – what the salmon fishing was like and whether he could recommend a comfortable hotel . . . .

Crusades or charades

The pilgrim, then, doesn't mind disaster – he courts it and usually gets the results he seeks. Even Tannhäuser's staff finally blossoms, though in the productions I see he never seems to come on to the stage the same side as he left for his penitential journey. 'Proof,' said my neighbour, an opera critic, 'if any were needed, that all roads lead *from* Rome.' We mustn't fail, though, to glance at the most definitively disastrous form of pilgrimage, certainly within the Western tradition – the Crusades. They all went wrong and, difficult though it is to select from such an *embarras de richesse* of catastrophe, my own choice has always been the Fourth Crusade, for its unbeatable mixture of misplaced spirituality, political chicanery, incompetence and sheer greed.

The crusade was instigated by Innocent III, one of the most powerful of medieval Popes and – this lamentable episode apart – one of the best organized. His aim was to go one better than Richard I by freeing the Holy Places permanently (Richard's feats of arms had merely secured permission for pilgrims to visit Jerusalem). To do this, Innocent prepared an attack first on Egypt, prophetically seen as the soft underbelly of Islam. Main problem – how to get there? There was by now (1202) only one way. Venetian sea power in the eastern Mediterranean was such that the whole project was inconceivable without the help of the *Serenissima*. Would Venice build a fleet and transport the crusaders? The aged Doge Enrico Dandolo announced that not only would she do so; he would accompany the expedition himself. He took the cross in an emotional ceremony in San Marco and the whole rich plum fell into Venetian hands.

A few months later a miscellaneous though predominantly French army ultimately numbering 20,000 was mustering in Venice, encamped well away from civilization on the Lido. Then, as now, the Venetians knew how to extract the last cent from the unwary tourist. They were well aware that most crusaders, especially at baronial level, were attracted to these expeditions not so much for the indulgences and other spiritual benefits they conferred but primarily because of the moratorium on all debts and interest occurring from them in the crusader's absence. Furthermore, the expedition, if successful, might well gain the participant booty, perhaps even lands and property – a new life. Hence it was worth going as liquid as possible. Even if you ultimately returned home defeated, your property was under Church protection. You had, in effect, nothing to lose. Even if you couldn't face actually going on the expedition yourself, it was perfectly common practice to take the crusade vow, gain the moratorium and then pay others to go in your stead.

A crusading army, therefore, included a high proportion of wealthy individuals, in temporary financial straits, who turned up with everything they could raise in terms of valuables as well as cash, their minds elsewhere, fixed on the prospect of a long and dangerous journey. Perfect victims for the hoteliers, the restaurateurs, the touts, the con men of the tourist industry, then as now. The Venetians set about relieving them of their assets with professional enthusiasm; indeed to such effect that the Doge was able to issue a new coin – the beautiful silver *grosso* backed by the precious objects the crusaders had been forced to hock to state-controlled pawnbrokers. Furthermore, since the Venetians were building the ships, they could control the entire time scale of the crusaders' stay. The ships were ready and waiting at the exact moment when it was calculated that the last crusader had finally run out of cash. We even know how much the Venetians were charging them at the end (prices had quadrupled – 'inflation'). 'Four marks per horse and two per man. It is an offence in the sight of God', one of the victims wrote.

Reader, if you have ever run out of money in Venice you will know the feeling. It *can't* be entirely one's fault. Somehow, somewhere along the line one has been robbed or at least taken for a ride. Desperate appeals to one's bank at home produce the promise of an immediate telex, yet day after day you go vainly to the Banco di Roma or the American Express office. '*Niente è arrivato, Signore*'. How can this be? Dreadful suspicions arise; they have lost the telex or are deliberately withholding it. They are forcing one to stay longer, to run up a bill in the *pensione*. They're all *in collusion* . . . . (Quite likely true. I have a friend who, informed by the manager of the Banco for fourteen consecutive days that his telex had not arrived, ripped the blotting paper off the top of that gentleman's desk crying, 'I bet it's *there!*' – and it was!)

Having reduced the crusaders to this perennial plight, the

'. . . in order to plant an Irish flag on top . . .'

Venetians now approached them with an offer they couldn't refuse. Their enormous debt as regards the ships would be commuted if the crusaders would consent to subdue the town of Zara, a troublesome port on the Dalmatian coast. Well, why not? They were getting off lightly and, anyway, the reduction of Zara would be a useful military exercise before the invasion of Egypt. Poor crusaders, 'travellers' to a man. How naïve can you get? Naturally the Venetians had no intention whatsoever of allowing this gang of military ruffians to sour their excellent commercial relations with the Sultan of Egypt. Even as the crusaders languished on the Lido, Doge Dandolo gave the Sultan his promise that the expedition would be deflected far from his shores. But it was not until after Zara had been successfully stormed that the crusaders were informed by their Venetian creditors where they were off to instead. To fight for the Cross, they were to storm Constantinople, the very heart of eastern Christianity.

Subsequent events show all concerned in the very basest light. Far from being shocked by this stupefying change of plan, the crusaders seem to have welcomed the idea of a campaign which would primarily involve looting the possessions of fellow Christians rather than trying to fight their way through ferocious Saracen armies to the unlootable Holy Places. Encouraged by the artful Dandolo, they overruled the Pope's frantic last-minute ban on this criminal attack, overcame the Emperor's feeble resistance and ran riot in the city for three days, in the course of which they destroyed any valuable work of art not already earmarked by the Venetian contingent for export to Venice (the four horses of San Marco, for instance). The expedition ended by destroying the last possible hope of reconciliation between the Greek and Latin churches, rendering homeless and bankrupt the majority of its participants, revealing as utterly futile Christian attempts to regain the Holy Land, undermining the authority of the Papacy, destroying, through the burning of libraries, a significant part of the Greek intellectual heritage, and finally bringing about, as a result of universal disillusion and disgust, one of the great medieval tragedies – the Children's Crusade. Quite a record, even as travel disasters go . . . .

Journey's End

Reader, I have offered you a significant *galère* of travellers. Most are the sort of people you would expect to get hopelessly mixed up travelling anyway – artists like James Reeve, beauties like Sarah (see p. 31) – but what of the kind of traveller you would assume to live in a world where such disasters don't even exist? Clearly such a person would be that doyen of film producers, Sam Spiegel. Spiegel was apparently capable of running out of money in the middle of Russia at a time when his dollar travellers' cheques were unacceptable (his personal assistant in London had to get him out of that by handing a somewhat bemused British Airways pilot £1000 in cash).

As for *The Bridge on the River Kwai*, our great producer decided – ah, fatal mistake! – to go one better than his director, David Lean, and bribed the explosives expert with the sum of £500 to blow the bridge up in an especially spectacular manner. The result of this unfortunate attempt to add yet more icing to the cake was that the bridge did not blow up at all, it simply collapsed into the river. Mr Spiegel was left in much the same situation as that of the director of the original *Ben Hur* who, after the chariot race, called out to his cameraman, 'Did you get it all?', and the reply came back, echoing across that vast Hollywood desert, 'OK, Sam, ready when you are.'

But may I allow Mr Spiegel to sum our travels up for us? The very first time he was in London, he tried to ask the way to the Tutankhamun exhibition. Like Oscar Wilde's Lord Henry, he speaks all modern languages fluently, but with so

'Should we fire first, or would you like to?'

strong an American accent that they all sound exactly the same. His request to be taken to 'Tuten Kharmen' came out to the taxi driver as 'Tooting Common'. Now I don't know if you have ever been to Tooting Common, especially on a very rainy Sunday morning. I personally haven't, but apparently it consists of an awful lot of trees, shrubs and grass; above all, it has no coherent geophysical existence. Can you imagine the world's most distinguished American film producer wandering helplessly around Tooting Common in the belief that somewhere there he was going to find the mummified body of Egypt's most sacred king . . . .

So, dear reader, I leave you alone after all these travel disasters. Would that I could come with you on your next trip, but how can I? The last time I set out it was, of course, for Venice, the travellers' ultimate dream. I ended up in Piacenza, and my luggage in Athens. Well, you know what the Australians say – life is a journey, not a destination. Good luck and *Bon voyage*.